To Mom from Dennis
Xmas 2002 ō love,

Toronto Sketches 5

D0669658

Toronto Sketches 5
"The Way We Were"

Mike Filey

Dundurn Press
Toronto • Oxford

Copyright © Mike Filey 1997

All rights reserved. No part of this publication may be reproduced, stored in a retrieval system, or transmitted in any form or by any means, electronic, mechanical, photocopying, recording, or otherwise (except for brief passages for purposes of review) without the prior permission of Dundurn Press Limited. Permission to photocopy should be requested from the Canadian Reprography Collective.

Editor: Barry Jowett
Designer: Scott Reid
Printer: Transcontinental Printing Inc.

Canadian Cataloguing in Publication Data

Filey, Mike, 1941-
    Toronto sketches 5: "the way we were"

ISBN 1-55002-292-X

1. Toronto (Ont.) — History.   I. Title

FC3097.4.F5492 1997   971.3'541   C97-931743-6
F1059.5.T6857F5492 1997

1 2 3 4 5 BJ 01 00 99 98 97

We acknowledge the support of the **Canada Council for the Arts** for our publishing program. We also acknowledge the support of the **Ontario Arts Council** and the **Book Publishing Industry Development Program** of the **Department of Canadian Heritage.**

THE CANADA COUNCIL | LE CONSEIL DES ARTS
FOR THE ARTS | DU CANADA
SINCE 1957 | DEPUIS 1957

Care has been taken to trace the ownership of copyright material used in this book. The author and the publisher welcome any information enabling them to rectify any references or credit in subsequent editions.

Printed and bound in Canada.

 Printed on recycled paper.

Dundurn Press   Dundurn Press   Dundurn Press
8 Market Street   73 Lime Walk   250 Sonwil Drive
Suite 200   Headington, Oxford   Buffalo, NY
Toronto, Ontario, Canada   England   U.S.A. 14225
M5E 1M6   OX3 7AD

Contents

Introduction

W hen I contributed my first column to the *Toronto Telegram*, little did I know that the newspaper was fast approaching its final deadline. In fact, on those random occasions when my views of Toronto, then and now, did appear, I was pretty sure that the presence of my material would send that particular day's circulation figures higher than they'd ever been. So you can imagine my astonishment when the news broke announcing that the Saturday, October 31, 1971 edition of the "Tely" would be the last. Could my columns have contributed to the untimely demise of what had become a true Toronto tradition?

Hardly. Seems the end was in sight (a fact that, at the time, was known to very few) long before I first approached Ray Biggart and Glenn Woodcock with the suggestion that the paper might wish to run a column using old photos of various parts of the city from my collection, contrasting them with the present-day views taken by *Telegram* photographers like Dick Loek or a young Norm Betts.

When the end did come, my connection with the *Telegram* had been insignificant. Nevertheless, my material had appeared in the *Toronto Telegram*, one of the country's great newspapers, and that fact was something I could always boast about.

The body was still warm when the *Toronto Sun* hit the newsstands early on Monday, November 1, 1971. As people warmed to "Toronto's Other Voice," as the new paper called itself, once again I was asked to be an "irregular" contributor (irregular in this case not referring to any medical condition, but rather indicating that my stuff wouldn't run every day or perhaps even every week. It would appear, well, irregularly.

Actually, it wasn't until some time after the Sunday edition of the paper first appeared in 1973 that my column, "The Way We Were," was to become a regular feature. Since then I'm proud to say that my column has been missing from the *Sunday Sun* on only one occasion — and that wasn't even my fault. The advertising people oversold the paper and I was bumped for a Crisco ad.

Toronto Sketches 5 contains columns that appeared in the *Sunday Sun* from August, 1995 through the end of December, 1996. The original publication date is provided at the beginning of each column. In some cases, additional material that may have been prompted by the column's first appearance has been incorporated in the book version. In addition, space limitations in the newspaper may have precluded the use of more than a couple of photos. Where applicable, those that were not used have been included in the book. Unless otherwise identified, all photos are from the author's collection. Special thanks goes to Irene at Charles Abel Photo Finishing for her assistance.

As always, people at the *Sun* have made my work that much easier and that much more fun. In particular I'd like to thank Marilyn Linton and Vena Eaton of the Lifestyle section and Ed Piwowarczyk at the Features Desk, each of whom ensures that my material actually makes it into the Sunday paper and looks good when it gets there. Researching material for each week's column results in extended periods in the *Sun's* library (tax man, please note). It could be a drag, but thanks to head librarian Julie Kirsh and her little helpers — Katherine, Glenna, Gillian, Joyce, and Sue — for both their help and tolerance. A special thanks to Jeff Rickard, one of the *Sun's* computer specialists whose expertise keeps my bits and bytes from running all over my RAM and ROM. By the way, Jeff now has his own business if you too need help.

Thanks also to the good people at Dundurn Press, who strive to turn out that vanishing breed of books — you know, the ones about our great country. It's a tough and often thankless job, but someone has to do it. Dundurn does it well.

And finally, I'm always on the lookout for story ideas as well as interesting old photographs of our city. If you have some of either and would like to share them with my *Sun* readers, drop me a note c/o the paper or the publisher.

Once again, thanks to my wife, proofreader, typist, and best fan, Yarmila.

Mike Filey
North York
(which after January 1, 1998 will
be Toronto).

SOME HIGH DRAMA ON EGLINTON AVE.

August 6, 1995

O ne sure way of telling that you are indeed getting old is to read that the Toronto Historical Board is about to place on its list of significant city structures a building that you actually watched being built when you were a kid. In my case the structure that's causing me some trauma is the former Union Carbide Building on Eglinton Avenue East between Yonge Street and Mt. Pleasant Road.

When I started my Grade 9 studies at North Toronto Collegiate in 1955 I was fortunate enough to get after-school and Saturday work as a drug peddler — or perhaps a better choice of words would be to say that I pedalled a delivery bike for Phil Lewis's Redpath Drug store at the northwest corner of Eglinton and Redpath avenues. (The building later became the site of the very first Golden Griddle restaurant.)

Across the street from the store was a row of old houses that were unceremoniously demolished in the fall of 1957 to make way for Union Carbide Canada Limited's new $5-million head office building. The building would be unique in that it was designed without interior columns, thereby creating huge, unobstructed floor areas on each of its eleven storeys.

Huge girders of the lofty Union Carbide Building litter Redpath Avenue following the collapse of the structure on September 6, 1958. Photo taken by seventeen-year-old drug store delivery boy Mike Filey.

By the summer of 1958 the substructure was complete and the building was beginning its skyward climb. Work was progressing smoothly and there was little reason to believe that staff couldn't start moving in sometime late the following year. Unfortunately, a small hitch was to change those plans.

On Saturday afternoon, September 6, 1958 the entire steel superstructure, all 1,800 tons of it, fell to the ground with a deafening roar. Many living

Now known as 123 Eglinton Avenue East, the building and adjacent parking lot are being redeveloped for condominiums and town houses.

nearby thought the Russians had finally dropped *the* bomb.

When the dust had settled, searchers were stunned to find no one was injured. The accident was due, no doubt, to the fact that the steelwork had collapsed on itself, although that's not to say there wasn't some damage done to nearby buildings. A few girders had hit the sidewalk on the Redpath side of the site, ricocheting off the concrete into a truck owned by Grierson the plumber, pushing it through the back wall of the garage. On the Eglinton Avenue side, a crane that had been perched on top of the steelwork hit the ground with such force that its boom shot out *under* the hydro wires, crashing onto a parked car and slicing it in half.

Although I wasn't working the day of the mishap I was soon at the site, attracted by both the noise and the news of the calamity, which had spread like wildfire through the entire community. Equipped with my small camera (I was just a poor student) I was able to convince the superintendent of the little three-storey apartment building kitty-corner to the remains of the

Union Carbide Building to let me go up on the roof to take the photo reproduced here. It was the first of hundreds of street scenes I've taken since that memorable day nearly thirty-seven years ago.

Subsequent examination of the site proved that the collapse was due, in part, to the building's unusual design. When workers left the still-unfinished structure the previous day it was assumed that "temporary" bracing would suffice until the last sections were put in place. That temporary bracing failed to withstand the unusually strong winds that developed during a brief but violent thunderstorm that roared through north Toronto that Saturday afternoon.

Once the site had been cleared of twisted and battered girders, design changes were made and construction began all over again. The building opened in June, 1960, one year behind schedule.

Today, Eglinton is one of the busiest streets in Metro, as anyone who spends time driving the city streets can confirm. Thirty-seven years ago traffic was a lot lighter and what might easily have been a major disaster was just an exciting photo opportunity for a seventeen-year-old delivery boy.

V-J Day: Fifty Years After the Agony

August 13, 1995

After nearly six traumatic years during which an estimated 54.8 million civilian and military personnel died (more than 40,000 of them Canadians), the Second World War came to an end, officially, exactly fifty years ago this coming Tuesday. And as decreed by US president Harry Truman that memorable day, August 15, 1945, would forever be known as V-J Day.

That's not to say that the entire world waited until the American president made it official to start victory celebrations. In fact, for most Canadians the final defeat of Germany a little more than three months earlier had already signalled the end of hostilities, simply because so many more men and women had served in Europe than in the Pacific.

Thus, by the time Truman's message announcing the end of the war in the Pacific theatre was flashed around the world, nearly three months had gone by since Canada had celebrated the end of "its" war on May 8, "V-E Day," with most of the country's military personnel either home from the European front or on their way.

But for many local families the war in the Pacific was still cause for concern with many wives and mothers anxiously awaiting news about the one thousand or more Canadian military personnel trapped in Japanese war camps where they had been held since the fall of Hong Kong on Christmas Day, 1941.

And for the 24,000 officers and men who had been posted to the Canadian Army's Pacific Force and were about to depart for jungle warfare training at Camp Breckenridge in Kentucky, the war was still very real.

(This part of Canada's commitment to help bring the "world" war to a victorious conclusion is of particular interest to me since my father decided to "stay in" after V-E Day and was actually en route to Kentucky [and to who knows what else] when "Little Boy" and "Fat Man" [the atomic bomb code names] were dropped on Hiroshima and Nagasaki.)

Like the army, both the RCN and RCAF had thousands of men on stand-by, just in case, while substantial numbers of Canadian naval and air force personnel remained in the Pacific war zone serving with Britain's navy and air

War-weary Torontonians "whoop it up" on V-E Day here in Toronto. V-J Day was still three agonizing months in the future. Recognize anyone in the photo?

force. Two RCN warships, *Uganda* and *Ontario*, were also on standby at Pacific Ocean bases, and large numbers of Canadian observers and technicians were still serving with the Allied armies in southeast Asia.

Following the end of the war in the Pacific, pandemonium once again erupted in Allied cities, though for reasons already explained Canadians celebrated with somewhat less enthusiasm than they had on V-E Day.

Unlike the German capitulation, which was decisive, the actual Japanese surrender took days to confirm. In fact, it was the premature belief that the war was over that resulted in a few people jumping the gun. One of these "eager beavers" was Canadian prime minister Mackenzie King, who on the night of August 12, two days early, helped confuse the situation when he took to the airwaves and announced that Japan had surrendered, basing his information on a United Press wire service report. This led, of course, to hundreds of Torontonians taking to the streets to celebrate, then retreating when King's error was announced.

Sheepishly, the president of the wire service offered a $5,000 reward for information leading to the identification and conviction of the person responsible for transmitting the so-called "false flash."

Once the "official" official announcement was made on August 14 crowds again took to the streets, and while for the most part activities were of the fun-loving variety the papers reported that some "hooliganism" occurred as gangs of youths roamed downtown streets smashing windows and setting bonfires. (And you thought only today's kids were bad.) The next day, rowdyism and hoopla turned to quiet contemplation as prayers for those who would never return were offered at religious services in city churches, and parks, and at the majestic cenotaph in front of City Hall.

Another three weeks were to go by before the proper documents were finally signed on board the *USS Missouri* in Tokyo Bay.

OLD TORONTO'S EXCELLENT ADVENTURE

August 20, 1995

Just as sure as there'll always be death, taxes, and politicians, so too will there always be the grand old lady of the waterfront, the Canadian National Exhibition. This annual event has been part of Toronto's history ever since the first fair, then known as the Toronto Industrial Exhibition, way back in the fall of 1879.

Over the years the focus of the Exhibition has changed dramatically. Today the emphasis is on providing fun and wholesome entertainment for the entire family, whereas in the fair's earliest years displays of the best crops and the newest agricultural implements along with displays of the latest in industrial and household inventions took precedence. In a world where the "state-of-the-art" in communications equipment was Alexander Graham Bell's remarkable contraption, the telephone, and "shopping malls" were limited to the dry goods emporiums of a few recent immigrants like Timothy Eaton and Robert Simpson, the "Ex" was an incredibly powerful magnet where people could come, see and touch.

The Crystal Palace, or Main Building, burned in 1906 and the Horticultural Building was erected on the site the following year.
Photo courtesy Marg Mossman

If we could go back in time, the following things would be among our discoveries at that very first Exhibition. The exact words used by newspaper reporters to describe the displays are shown in quotations.

Let's wander the grounds. Over at the Main Building (which stood where the Horticultural Building is today and was also known as the Crystal Palace) there's "a very choice collection of Prussian dried grasses and flowers consisting of bouquets, wreaths and mantle pieces." Nearby Messrs. Sears of Toronto (no, not that Sears) is exhibiting a *Bijou* writing desk christened the "Princess Louise" (in honour of the wife of the governor general of the day). It measures but 1 foot 6 inches by 2 feet and is made out of walnut with "no less than 200 feet of the finer ornamental woods used in its manufacture." The paper went on to suggest that "the tenth commandment will be frequently broken while it is undergoing inspection by the ladies." (By the way, in case you've forgotten, that's the one about coveting things.) There's also a large display of sealskin carriage rugs, bearskin and wolverine robes, and ladies muffs, one variety formed out of "the lustrous plumage surmounted by the head and bill of the Indian pheasant."

A Montreal firm is exhibiting displays of their fruit extracts, including some Limetta Cordial, the flavour of which was "suggestive of bright skies, feathery palm trees and murmurs of the ocean." Wow!! Gimme a gallon.

Under the dome in the Crystal Palace, c.1900.

Behind this exhibit is the booth of Windsor, Ontario's Globe Tobacco Works where "no less than 50 varieties of the gentle weed" are on view. Along the way Christie, Brown and Company are showing three hundred varieties of fancy biscuits while Mr. Webb's wedding cakes are being viewed "by eager young ladies and bashful young men."

In the popular Machinery Hall, the Thomson and Williams Manufacturing company has eight varieties of harvesting machines on view, including the model that carried off first prize at an international test exhibition at Paris, France the previous year. Nearby the Haggart Brothers proudly display their patented dustless separator, a hard straw cutter, the Tiger sulky rake, and the unchokeable Royce reaper. There's also an undershot clover mill, several reapers and mowers (plus a combination reaper/mower), and a grain harvester available in both horse and steam power models. (Little do the makers know that before long all their products will be surpassed by those turned out by newcomer Hart Massey, who is in the process of moving his factory from Newcastle, Ontario to a new site just north of the Exhibition grounds.)

Looking for some patio furniture, or whatever they call the stuff in the nineteenth century? The Belle Ewart Rustique Company have a nice display of their wares. And for those who need one, over there is an Oxford glass hen house.

Oh, when you visit the fair be sure to see the CNE Archives exhibit in the Music Building. This year the exhibit highlights the Ex and the war years.

AIR SHOWS TAKE "EX" TO THE SKY

August 27, 1995

Without doubt, one of the most popular attractions at each year's Exhibition is the Canadian International Air Show, which has been held on the fair's final long weekend for almost forty years. This year's show will be held on September 2, 3 and 4 (weather permitting) commencing each day at 1:30 pm.

We can trace the origins of the annual air show in Toronto to the 1919 CNE when a number of Fokker D VII fighter bi-planes thrilled the crowds with "daring formation flying over the waterfront." To be sure, Torontonians had seen planes both on the ground and in the air long before the 1919 CNE display. Historically, it was Count Jacques de Lesseps' remarkable flight over the city in 1910, conducted as part of that year's pioneer aviation show at a makeshift airfield northwest of the Keele/Eglinton intersection, that could be interpreted as Toronto's first "air show" of any kind.

This very rare photo of Capt. Knabenshue's Air Ship lifting off on its ill-starred flight was given to me years ago by a reader. The photo was a mystery until I came across the story of the accident in the August 29, 1907 edition of the *Evening Telegram* in the *Sun* library collection.

With the outbreak of war in Europe literally minutes away the 1939 CNE tried to pump up their patrons' jingoism by inviting the RCAF to put on a display. High over the grounds fifteen Oxford light bombers, one Hurricane, one Lysander (Toronto-built), and six Fairey Battles thrilled the crowds — not a few of whom would rush down to the recruiting office the next day to sign up.

Once the war was over, air shows began to be held on an annual basis under the auspices of the National Aeronautical Association first at de Havilland and Malton (now Pearson) airports with periodic appearances at the Exhibition grounds, though never during the fair. That didn't happen until 1956.

Now, having documented the lineage of today's air shows, I must include a comment about a little known and less-than-successful attempt at an "air show" at the Ex back in 1907. It was in that year that Exhibition officials eagerly announced the appearance, direct from Buffalo, New York, of "Capt. Knabenshue's Air Ship" which would "take flight daily at 5 pm."

The craft consisted of a huge cigar-shaped gas bag, fifty-three feet in length and eighteen feet at its greatest diameter, made of Japanese silk coated with varnish. At the stern of the gas bag was a large rudder made of bamboo and covered in more treated silk.

Suspended under the bag was a steel frame to which was attached a small gasoline engine driving a pair of screw propellers located at the stern of the strange craft. The pilot (back then referred to as the navigator) was Mr. Gail Robinson, who rode the contraption like a bike, sliding to the back of the frame to make it rise and to the front to make it fall. He claimed the craft could do 60 mph, "in a dead calm."

The lifting gas was hydrogen — cubic feet of it (generated by pouring sulfuric acid on iron filings) — a fact that prompted the navigator, when asked if he was going to take anyone up with him on his flight, to answer "all you fellows around me if that man over by the gas pipes keeps smoking his pipe."

Although operation of the craft was extremely dependent on weather conditions, the contract nevertheless called for the air ship to go up after four consecutive days, regardless of those conditions. So it was that on August 29, 1907 navigator Robinson took off. The wind caught the unmanageable craft, carrying it due north right into the belfry on top of the old public school at the corner of Crawford and King streets.

Robinson was only slightly damaged, his craft more so. Exhibition officials were irate. Several days later, the final news account of this abortive "air show" went like this:

The Knabenshue air ship has made another flight, the last she will probably make from the Exhibition grounds. The flight was not by the power of her own engine, but by the aid of a horse and wagon. Early on Sunday morning the air ship was loaded on the dray and conveyed to the Parkdale railway station.

*   *   *   *   *

While on the subject of air shows, how'd you like to win one of a dozen authentic flight suits donated by crews of Royal Air Force's Nimrod, our own Snowbirds, and others. All proceeds will go to the Hospital for Sick Children and #180 Mosquito Squadron, Royal Canadian Air Cadets. The tickets ($2 each or three for $5) will be available at the air show, at the popular Pearson Airport "Walk- About," or by calling (416) 481-3025.

Less than a week after this column ran, a Nimrod of the Royal Air Force crashed into Lake Ontario while participating in the 1995 edition of the Canadian International Air Show. Seven young crew members died.

A LOOK BACK AT THE "EX"

September 3, 1995

As the 117th edition of the CNE gets set to close up shop for another year, it's an opportune time to examine how this popular Canadian tradition has changed over the years. Today's Exhibition has evolved into an eighteen-day festival of family entertainment. And although there may be a few similarities, the modern-day focus is far removed from the vision fostered by the fair's founding fathers.

The Ex was born in an era when words like radio, television, and shopping centre weren't to be found in any dictionary. From the start, the Toronto Industrial Exhibition (to give the event its original name) was *the* place to view the newest, most modern agricultural implements and industrial inventions, as well as the products that these remarkable creations had made possible. As the years passed the importance of the CNE as the place to have new products introduced to the public increased until it became, quite literally, "the Showplace of the Nation."

Even the names of the fair's exhibit buildings reflected the importance placed on the inventive genius of Canadians: the Stove Building, the Farm Implements Building, the Carriage Building, the Machinery Hall, the Dairy Building, and even the Fruit Building.

Before long "horseless carriage" makers were offered space at the fair to exhibit this new-fangled (and not yet universally accepted) mode of transportation. Initially, the automobile was allocated room in a structure with the rather generic title of Transportation Building. Alongside were motorboats, bicycles, and a selection of "infernal flying machines." As the years went by the planes all but vanished (to return as an important element of the annual CNE in 1956), but the cars became important enough to have their own special palace. The new Automotive Building, erected in a mere 138 days, opened in 1929. In the years that followed hundreds of new models, including the "Tucker," the "Jeepster," and the "Edsel" were introduced to the car-driving public at the annual fair.

Even Canada's trio of major railroad companies (Grand Trunk, Canadian Pacific, and Canadian Northern) recognized the importance of being represented at the Ex, getting together in 1907 to sponsor a new Railway

Building, which was designed to accommodate each company's exhibits, and included a diorama display in one of the building's three lobes. The structure later became the Music Building, and is now the Wintario Pavilion.

What was to become one of the Ex's most popular buildings was the Electrical and Engineering Building. Erected in 1928 on the north side of Princes' Boulevard (on a site soon to be occupied by the new National Trade Centre), it was in this massive building that Canadians were introduced to the newest in ranges, refrigerators, radios, television receivers (first demonstrated in front of Canadian audiences at the 1939 Ex), high fidelity phonograph systems, and stereophonic sound.

The previewing of the marvels of electricity had been one of the fair's earliest triumphs, the grounds having been illuminated with arc lights in 1882, making it the first fair in the world to do so.

A couple of years later the electric street railway was pioneered at the Ex, followed by the introduction of the now-familiar trolley wheel and pole in 1885, another world first. Since then, numerous new TTC models have met the riding public for the first time at the annual fair.

In 1925, a young Toronto inventor introduced his revolutionary new AC-powered radio to amazed fair-goers. No

This ad from September 9, 1925 *Evening Telegram* invited the world to discover Ted Roger's new "batteryless" radio at the 1925 CNE.

Digging the tunnel for the Yonge Street subway had just started when this idea of what Canada's first subway train would look like was presented on the Grandstand stage at the 1950 CNE.

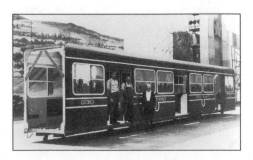

longer would listeners be burdened with cumbersome, acid-filled "A" and "B" batteries. Now, ordinary house current could provide the power. As a matter of fact, the Standard Radio Manufacturing Company's slogan said it all: "Just plug in, then tune in. That's all." And twenty-five-year-old Ted Rogers had chosen the Ex as the place to introduced his batteryless radio to the world. Less than two years later, Rogers' new radio station CFRB ("RB" for Rogers batteryless) went on the air.

Communications was always an important component of the fair's list of annual attractions. Pedro, the world's first machine capable of reproducing the human voice (developed in the Bell Telephone laboratories), thrilled visitors to the 1941 CNE.

Then along came trade shows, consumer shows, the Convention Centre, SkyDome, and mammoth shopping malls, and the CNE changed. For better? For worse? Who knows. The grand old lady just changed.

T.O.'s "New" City Hall Turns 30

September 10, 1995

Hands up all those who remember when "Help" by The Beatles topped the record charts, or when the "prime time" TV stars were "Perry Mason," "Gomer Pyle," "Dr. Kildare," and "Hazel." Perhaps you can recall the night you went to the Odeon Carlton theatre to see Michael Caine in "The Ipcress File," or the time you travelled out into the suburbs to see Burt Lancaster and Lee Remick ride down "The Hallelujah Trail" at the Glendale Theatre, "the home of Canada's biggest, brightest cinerama screen." (By the way, both those picture houses have been demolished, as have many of their contemporaries: University, Alhambra, Palace, Odeon Fairlawn, etc., etc. Even the old Loew's and Imperial theatres have been renamed the Elgin and Pantages, respectively.)

Or perhaps you can recall when it was "in" to visit Toronto's numerous coffee houses, places like the Bohemian Embassy on St. Nicholas Street or the Mousehole and Riverboat in Yorkville, where the entertainment was provided by performers such as Jim McHarg, Joso and Malka, the Lords of London, and Jesse Colin Young.

If any of these suggestions bring back memories I hope you're sitting down for this next one, because it was while all these things were going on that a building that has evolved into one of Toronto's most distinguished landmarks was officially opened. The year, 1965; the building, "New" City Hall. That's right, "New" City Hall will be thirty years old next Wednesday!

While the building was new in 1965, the idea of a new city hall for the city wasn't. In fact, it was just a few years after what is now regarded as "old" City Hall opened in 1899 that the city fathers began voicing the need for a new building, as the old one was already overcrowded.

However, it wasn't until the early 1950s that talk turned into action with the first substantive plans taking shape late in 1955 in the form of a rather nondescript $18-million, twenty-storey office building complete with a roof garden restaurant. This city hall, sitting on eleven acres of what had been proposed for decades as the community's future "civic square", a site that we know today as Nathan Phillips Square, would serve city departments and politicians as well as the governmental needs of the recently created Municipality of Metropolitan Toronto.

Later that same year, when the question of a new city hall was put to the electorate on the civic ballot, the proposal was soundly defeated. The question was rewritten for 1956 (with the original $18-million estimate for construction massaged down to "a net cost of $13.5 million for both erecting and equipping" — *Dear reader, keep this figure in mind as you read on*).

This time the idea was approved. Toronto would get its new city hall. It was then decided that rather than limit the ultimate look of this important civic project to the creative minds of just Canadian architects, the venture would be open to architects world-wide.

On September 26, 1958, after sifting through more than five hundred submissions from architects in forty-two different countries (and, incidentally by the narrowest of votes, with the two dissenting voices warning that the

The city's stately Registry Building would soon be demolished as work on the new City Hall and the yet-unnamed civic square progresses in the summer of 1964.

winning design would cost more than the budgeted figure — *keep this in mind, too*), the "go ahead" was given to proceed with the unusual concept put forward by forty-two-year-old Finnish architect Viljo Revell. The first sod was turned, the cornerstone laid, and on September 13, 1965, thirty years ago Wednesday and almost a year later than planned, "New" City Hall was officially opened by Governor General Georges Vanier. Oh, the final cost of the $13.5-million structure? Who knows? Something over $30 million some say, a figure more than twice that original estimate. An all-too-familiar story.

THE YOUNG TRAIN MAN WHO COULD

September 17, 1995

On first glance the accompanying photo seems simply to portray an old locomotive complete with its nattily attired two-man crew posing for the camera during a coffee break (or whatever kind of break they took in those far-off days). In fact this view has become much more interesting to me since reading a copy of the Summer, 1986 edition of *The York Pioneer*, a dandy little booklet published annually by the York Pioneer and Historical Society. (You can contact the society at P.O. Box 45026, 2482 Yonge Street, Toronto M4P 3E3.)

One of the stories included in that issue of the *Pioneer* was written by Philip Creighton and deals with the life and times of John Harvie, who just happens to be the gentleman seen leaning against the cowcatcher at the left of the old photo.

Harvie, who was born in Scotland in 1833 and emigrated to North America in 1851, was certainly a multi-faceted person, sort of a man for all seasons. After a short stint in Toledo, Ohio he ventured across the border and on to the small city of Toronto, population approximately 31,000.

John Harvie (left) and W.H. Anderson (near cab) pose with steam locomotive *Lady Elgin* on the railway's right-of-way near the foot of Brock Street (renamed Spadina Avenue) c.1853.

All his working life, Harvie had demonstrated an interest in the fascinating new world of ship and railway transportation, so it wasn't out of character for the young man to seek out a position with the newly-established Ontario, Simcoe and Huron Railway which was in the process of constructing the province's first rail line northward from the young provincial capital to a proposed terminus on Georgian Bay, near the present community of Collingwood. The company's belief in the business prospects afforded by its new steam railway was reflected in the choice of the company name that listed each of the lakes which it planned to serve. Before long, however, the name was streamlined to the more compact Northern Railway.

Actual construction of this pioneer line began on October 15, 1851 when Lady Elgin, the wife of Queen Victoria's representative in the United Canadas (as Ontario and Quebec were known prior to Confederation) turned the ceremonial first sod on the water's edge not far from the main entrance to Toronto's present Union Station. To honour this historic occasion the company christened its first locomotive *Lady Elgin*, which some royalists might have interpreted as an anti-British gesture since the engine had been built in the United States of America. Following the ceremony *Lady Elgin*, the locomotive not the Governor-in-Chief's wife, resumed its task of helping to build the new rail line. It is, in fact, the locomotive seen in the accompanying photo.

As the first day of operation approached someone had to be selected from the company ranks to act as conductor. Harvie had been in charge of ticket sales so it was natural that he would have been chosen to board and take charge of the inaugural run that chugged out of the little station on May 15, 1853. As the line was still far from completion, the temporary terminus was to be at a place called Matchell's Corners (now Aurora).

A greater honour was to befall Harvie, for in 1860 he was put in charge of a special train conveying the popular Prince Edward, Queen Victoria's eldest son and heir to the throne, on an outing from Toronto, where the young man had just dedicated Queen's Park, to Collingwood and a boat cruise on the bay. On the return trip, between the Thornhill and Weston stations, the royal train reached the incredible speed of 55 mph.

In 1878, Harvie was appointed station master of Toronto's new Union Station. Three years later, and after twenty-eight years in the railway business, the forty-eight-year-old John Harvie resigned. In 1884 he served one term as city alderman for St. Patrick's Ward and in the following year was elected a trustee for the Toronto General Burying Ground, just in time to participate in the trust's plan to acquire and develop the new Prospect Cemetery out at dusty St. Clair Avenue in the city's western countryside.

On September 5, 1917 John Harvie passed away and two days later was buried in Mt. Pleasant Cemetery.

HOSPITAL ALMOST FUNDING CASUALTY

September 24, 1995

Most people are aware that much of the medical profession here in Canada is presently under intense scrutiny by various levels of government and changes to the system are obviously in the works. Closer to home, local hospitals too are facing new prospects as long-standing mandates and priorities are changed. All this reminds me of the following headline that appeared in a city newspaper:

TORONTO HOSPITAL CLOSES OVER LACK OF MONEY.

While this may read like something from some recent edition, the words actually refer to a situation that paralyzed much of Toronto's medical fraternity more than a century-and-a-quarter ago.

Early in 1868 city hospital operating expenses began to climb higher than all available sources of income. This situation eventually resulted in an announcement by the trustees of the city's only hospital, the Toronto General

Postcard view of the old hospital's sprawling successor that opened on College Street in 1913, by which time Toronto's population had mushroomed to well over 400,000.

Sketch of Toronto's first General Hospital erected on the northwest corner of King and John streets when our city was still just a town with a population of only 3,000.

(which back then was located on Gerrard Street near the Don River) explaining that the financial situation had become intolerable and effective immediately the facility would be forced to close its doors to the general public.

And while the situation was certainly disconcerting for the community's 49,000 citizens (as well as to many patients from the outlying suburban areas) the announcement finally brought things to a head. Before long new sources of funding were in place and the General was able to reopen its wards and operating rooms on October 7 of the following year.

The Toronto General Hospital (which in recent years has become affiliated with the Western Hospital to form the Toronto Hospital, Metro's largest) has a long and fascinating history. But interestingly, its origins really have more to do with our community's short but violent war with the United States in 1812–14 than to the presence of any combinations of maladies afflicting its citizens.

Not long after President Madison's troops launched the first of many assaults on peaceful Canadian settlements an organization called the Loyal and Patriotic Society was convened in York (Toronto). One of the society's mandates was to search out sources of money and goods to help victims of these unprovoked attacks.

As it turned out, more than enough money was raised to permit the construction of a small hospital just north of the Garrison (Fort York) where wounded soldiers could receive attention. Three years after hostilities ended, efforts turned to the construction of a hospital to administer to the needs of the general citizen population. While some money was available, more was needed and it came from a rather unexpected source.

With the war successfully concluded, the Loyal and Patriotic Society decided to strike a number of medals that would be awarded to the "heroes of the war." Unfortunately (for the heroes) the proposed distribution of these gold and silver medals got so caught up in the politics of the day that it was eventually decided not to award any of them. Rather, the medals were to be defaced and sold for approximately $2,000, the value of the precious metals. This money was then added to the amount already on hand for the construction of a public infirmary. A site at the northwest corner of King and John streets was selected, though the original plan was to erect the structure somewhere on today's Richmond Street (which explains the choice of that thoroughfare's original name, Hospital Street). Although construction began in 1820, the process was painfully slow. In fact, just as the two-storey brick building was finally ready for occupation more than five years later, the building was suddenly commandeered by government officials for use as a temporary Parliament Building, the real one having just been destroyed by fire.

Patients didn't actually get access to the new facility until 1829, after which time the building remained in use for twenty-seven years before a new, larger General Hospital opened on Gerrard Street to serve a population that had grown from 3,000 in 1830 to more than 40,000 in 1856.

The first buildings of the present hospital complex on College Street at University opened in 1913.

THE SAGA OF THE O'KEEFE CENTRE

October 1, 1995

A couple of weeks ago I commented in this column on how difficult is was to believe that Toronto's "new" City Hall celebrated its thirtieth anniversary on September 13. Well, if you found that piece of information hard to believe here's another morsel of Toronto trivia that's just as astounding.

It was on this very day thirty-five years ago that the O'Keefe Centre officially opened with the world premier of Alan Jay Lerner and Frederick Loewe's *Camelot* with Julie Andrews, Richard Burton, and Roddy McDowall in the starring roles. The show also introduced a young Canadian-trained, American-born Robert Goulet as Lancelot.

To be historically accurate, the theatre actually saw its first audience the previous evening when a full dress rehearsal of the new play thrilled staff members of the O'Keefe Brewing Company and their families, plus dozens of local tavern owners and inn keepers. In fact, it was this very association with the beer business that nearly scuttled Toronto Mayor Nathan Phillips' plan to get a civic auditorium for his city, at no cost.

As part of Phillips' campaign leading up to the 1955 municipal election, he voiced his concern that, as up-to-date as the City of Toronto might appear, it had no public auditorium for the use of its citizens, visitors to the city, or convention groups. One of his priorities, if elected, would be to obtain such a facility, and to do so at little or no cost to the city.

Just days after being elected Toronto's new mayor, Phillips received a letter from the president of the O'Keefe Brewing Company in which M.J. Kelly stated that, in response to the mayor's concerns about the lack of a civic auditorium, the O'Keefe Company, through the yet-to-be-established O'Keefe Centre Foundation, would be prepared to spend between $10 million and $12 million on such a facility, conditional on the city providing a suitable location in the central downtown area at cost.

The letter went on, "Our company was established in Toronto in 1846 and for the intervening 109 years it has been an enthusiastic and staunch supporter of all causes beneficial to the city and its people."

The offer appeared to be just what the mayor was seeking. With its

It was for Eugene O'Keefe, and not the beer, that the O'Keefe Centre was originally named, or so they claimed.

Front Street looking west to Yonge from Scott Street, 1951. The old buildings on the south side of Front were demolished for the new O'Keefe Centre.

acceptance he could quickly fulfill his first election promise. This was going to be easy. Or was it?

Just hours after the offer was made public, and while officials were still discussing where to locate the new building (should it be opposite the new city hall? [today's Sheraton Centre site] or perhaps at the southwest corner of College and University? [the Ontario Hydro head office]), a few naysayers began to voice their disapproval of having a civic facility not only funded by, but named in recognition of ... a brewing company!

Resistance to the name selection was pretty much stifled when the opponents were reminded that Eugene O'Keefe, founder of the company, had been one of Toronto's earliest and most generous philanthropists, long associated with the support of religious, philanthropic, educational, and welfare projects. And on the subject of welfare, the company seemed to defuse any further opposition when it announced that any and all profits generated by the new auditorium would be turned over to "meritorious welfare organizations" while all losses would be absorbed by the company. A brief verbal skirmish arose when someone suggested that competition from the new O'Keefe Auditorium (a proposed name that never materialized) would adversely affect the rentability of the new Women's Building proposed for the Exhibition grounds.

When the Front and Yonge site for the new auditorium was finally chosen it looked like clear sailing ahead. No such luck.

A request by the company that the city give up title to a small lane that ran through the south part of the property caused a few politicians to balk. Fortunately, difficulties over that lane, which was valued at a mere $60,000, didn't kill the $12-million project.

On June 14, 1958, nearly three years after the offer to build a civic auditorium was originally made, the first steel was finally put in place. The new O'Keefe Centre opened on October 1, 1960 and was purchased by Metro Toronto for $2.7 million eight years later. On November 30, 1996, the auditorium's name was officially changed to the Hummingbird Centre for the Performing Arts. Hummingbird Communications Ltd. is a Canadian software development company that has undertaken long-term sponsorship of the facility.

The O'Keefe Centre as depicted in a 1962 postcard view.

EVERYTHING OLD IS NEW — AGAIN

October 8, 1995

I n 1906 the Hydro Electric Power Commission of Ontario (since 1974, Ontario Hydro) was created by the provincial government, with the concurrence and enthusiastic support of many local municipalities, as a way of ensuring that electrical power would be available to the citizens at the lowest possible cost. Up until that time (and for a number of years after) electricity was generated and distributed by private concerns, and in the process generated great quantities of money for the principles of those companies. Perhaps the best known Toronto personality to make a bundle from the sale of electrical power was Sir Henry Pellatt, with much of his money going towards building Casa Loma.

The creation of a public body to look after the power needs of the young

North Yonge Railways car #410 southbound entering Hogg's Hollow. The bridge in the background was built in 1929 (construction took just nine months) as the extension of Yonge Boulevard over the Don Valley, allowing Yonge Street traffic to skirt the dangerous, and frequently impassable Hogg's Hollow hill. The bridge connected with Yonge Street near today's Highway 401 interchange. Years later the bridge was incorporated into the Highway 401 crossing of this same ravine.

province was welcomed by almost everyone (except the "power barons," of course). Gratuitous stories filled the newspapers of the day and Adam Beck, the driving force behind this new electric commission, was eventually knighted for his efforts.

Nearly nine decades have gone by and, wouldn't you know it, Hydro's once again in the news, though this time for a very opposite reason. There are rumblings that Ontario Hydro may be … privatized! Sir Adam must be spinning in his Hamilton, Ontario grave. In fact, I believe I heard some uncomplimentary epithets emanating from his statue on University Avenue the other day.

Hydro was also a big news item in the days following the end of the Second World War, but for a totally different reason. With the return of prosperity it soon became painfully apparent that the province was running short of electrical power. Certainly new power plants were in the works, but it would take time to get them "on stream." Power generated outside Ontario was purchased, but even this wasn't sufficient to combat the ever-increasing shortages. Eventually it became necessary to ration how much electricity would be fed into the various power grids that served different parts of the province. This often resulted in certain areas experiencing what were termed "brown outs." Even worse were the actual cuts in electricity when all power would be shut off, occasionally for as long as forty-five minutes.

As a major electrical consumer, the Toronto Transportation Commission decided to do its bit by eliminating two streetcar routes: the downtown

Inauguration of the North Yonge Railways service at the city limits, Yonge Street and Glen Echo (now the site of a mammoth Loblaw's store), July 17, 1930.

Spadina line (operating between Fleet Street, renamed Lake Shore Boulevard a dozen years later, and Bloor Street) and the North Yonge line that had survived as a remnant of the once-popular radial line. (The radial line, so called as it radiated northward from the city, connected the northern terminus of the Yonge city streetcar line with rural communities along Yonge Street [Willowdale, Lansing, Newtonbrook, Thornhill, Richmond Hill, Aurora, and Newmarket]. At its zenith the "Metropolitan" ran all the way to Sutton and Jackson's Point on Lake Simcoe.)

The Spadina line had an "ancient" history, having been inaugurated as a horsecar route in the 1870s. This line will be reactivated as the "new" Spadina LRT route in 1997. (Perhaps I'm going out on a limb with this statement considering what's happened recently with the two new subway projects.)

The North Yonge line had actually been terminated once before as a result of drastic reductions in passenger and freight traffic as automobiles and highway coaches became more and more popular modes of transportation. Just four months after the March 15, 1930 termination, pressure from some of the communities along the route resulted in operations being resumed as far north as Richmond Hill. The resurrection of what was now known as the North Yonge Railways kept streetcar service going until the hydro dilemma of 1948 resulted in final termination. The last radials on Yonge trundled into the Eglinton car house early on the morning of October 10, 1948 (forty-seven years ago this coming Tuesday), the long-familiar whine of their electric motors replaced by the growl (and fumes) of diesel buses engines. Incidentally, one of these radial cars, #416, (built in 1925 and converted into a "dwelling" when retired in 1948) can still be seen at the Halton County Radial Railway Museum near Guelph, Ontario.

TTC WOES REMINDER OF EARLIER TIMES

October 22, 1995

T he dissension that's become all-too-evident in recent weeks between the Toronto Transit Commission and newly elected members of the provincial government is certainly not a new phenomenon. This time the debate is over the amount of government money available for day-to-day operations and whether there's enough money in the till for one, two, or any new subway lines. But government intrusion into the field of public transit is nothing new, as the following headline proves:

DOUBT QUEEN'S PARK WILL IMPEDE SUBWAY CONSTRUCTION

Sounds like something that appeared in a recent edition of the paper, doesn't it? Actually the words ran in the August 12, 1949 *Evening Telegram* and headed up a story that described the possibility of the Ontario Municipal Board stepping in to prevent the TTC from building the city's first subway, the Yonge line.

Seems that the question put to the voters in early 1945 as to whether the subway should be built at all included a statement that the project would only go ahead if federal funding to the tune of twenty percent of the total cost (then estimated at $35 million, a figure that was to escalate to $60 million) was agreed upon by Ottawa officials.

With voter approval overwhelming, but not a dollar forthcoming from Ottawa and construction about to start, the *Telegram* wondered aloud whether the provincial government might step in at the last minute and stop the TTC from proceeding with the project. While government interference was a definite concern, no such action was taken. Work proceeded and Toronto's first subway opened on March 30, 1954.

But there have been other occasions where the province has actually attempted to advance the cause of public transit only to have its well-intentioned plans "derailed."

The most celebrated was a scheme worth $1.3 billion put forward by Ontario Premier Bill Davis in 1972 (the year after the cancellation of the

In 1973 an artist portrayed a Krauss-Maffei magnetic levitation train approaching the Ontario Place station on the experimental Exhibition Place elevated rapid transit line. Switching problems "derailed" the project.
Photo credit: Ontario Ministry of Transportation and Communications.

celebrated Spadina Expressway) that proposed modern, high-speed trains rushing between stations on elevated tracks in three traffic-clogged Ontario cities — Toronto, Hamilton and Ottawa — with our city getting a total of seventy-five miles of track, most of it supported eight feet in the air on massive concrete pillars. The plan was to have elevated trains running to the airport from Islington and Bloor, east from downtown along the waterfront to Kennedy and Eglinton, and over Finch Avenue from Highway 400 to Port Union Road.

Nine firms, including Hawker-Siddeley, Ford, and Krauss-Maffei, were asked to submit proposals for the construction and operation of a two-mile-long experimental test facility down at the Exhibition grounds. The K-M concept, featuring the noiseless, vibrationless (and as yet unproven) principle of magnetic levitation as the vehicle's motive source, won the contract.

"Work on the project will commence following the conclusion of the 1973 CNE," stated the CNE's then-GM David Garrick. The province chimed in that it had no doubt that the system would be operational in time for the 1975 edition of the fair. Well, at least Dave's statement turned out to be correct. The construction phase did begin as promised, but by late 1974 it was evident that the project, now dubbed GO-Urban and estimated to have cost in excess of $25 million, was going nowhere, both literally and figuratively. Seems that switching difficulties on tracks covered with ice (not an unknown occurrence during Toronto winters, especially down by the lake) had become a major, major problem. By the end of the year the provincial government's venture into the world of public transit was, for all intents and purposes, dead, at least for the time being.

* * * * *

Historical Walking Tour of Kew Beach, a new fifty-six-page booklet written by Mary Campbell and Barbara Myrvold that features descriptions and photos of twenty-four Kew Beach sites, is now available from the Toronto Public Library's Beaches, Main, and Northern branches for $8 (plus GST) or by mail. Call 416-393-7535 for further details.

* * * * *

Rochester reader Robert Sawyer wonders if any recordings of the Luigi Romanelli Orchestra exist. If you know of any drop me a line here at the *Sun*. Born in Belleville, Ontario in 1885, young Luigi performed with numerous pit orchestras in several "pre-talkie" Toronto movie houses. In 1923 Romanelli and his newly formed orchestra were frequently heard (and danced to) at Toronto's King Edward Hotel and at the Manoir Richelieu in Murray Bay, Quebec where Luigi died in 1942. His brothers, Don and Leo, were also well-known local musicians, the former as conductor of dance bands on board the popular Lake Ontario steamers *Cayuga* and *Chippewa*.

Oh, Island in the Scheme...

October 29, 1995

R eaders of this column will be aware that stories I enjoy relating are those that have to do with history repeating itself. You know, things that are passed off as brand new today when, in fact, it's all been tried, or at the very least, talked about before. Take for instance the recent decision by Toronto City Council to proceed with a "fixed link" that will physically connect Toronto Island with the mainland. A new suggestion? Hardly.

One of the earliest suggestions to connect the city with Toronto Island was made by one of the city's numerous committees ninety-nine years ago when it proposed that streetcar service to the island be inaugurated. To do so, the committee recommended that Bathurst Street be pushed south of Front (where it ended) crossing the existing railway corridor on a long viaduct that

A rare photograph showing work starting on the "fixed-link" to Toronto Island, September, 1935. Within a month the tunnel project was dead. Note the old Maple Leaf ball stadium to the left and the chimney and watertank at the present Channel 47 studio site at the Bathurst/Lake Shore intersection.

would continue southward, passing over the Western Channel via a swing bridge. Streetcars would run from the King/Bathurst corner, over the channel, south to a point near the lighthouse, then curve eastward running along the south shoreline of the island to a loop near the Eastern Channel. The cost of the project? Approximately $150,000, $60,000 of which was for the swing bridge, or "fixed link" to use today's terminology.

Obviously nothing happened, but that didn't stop a continuous flow of ideas for a connection between the city and its island. In 1909 Parks Commissioner Wilson envisioned an automobile-only driveway following a route similar to that proposed for streetcars thirteen years earlier. Seems the commissioner believed streetcars and parks weren't compatible while cars and parks were. In his plan the crossing of the channel would be accomplished via a sixteen-foot-wide tunnel. This appears to be the first time that access to the island via a tunnel was suggested. Again, nothing happened.

When the newly created Harbour Commission presented its comprehensive waterfront redevelopment plan in 1912, once again bridges were back in vogue — only this time there was to be a pair of them bridging the channels at either end of the island. In addition, five others were proposed over various island lagoons, thereby permitting the construction of a motor boulevard (complete with massive 1,034 car parking lot) that would encircle the island.

Interestingly, the island drive was to be just a segment of a much larger highway project that would ultimately encircle the entire city. Today's Lake Shore Boulevard west of Bathurst Street is all that came of this incredibly farsighted scheme.

When plans for an airport at the west end of the island were presented in the mid-1930s a tunnel under the channel was considered an absolute necessity. As a result, on August 6, 1935 the city's powerful Board of Control requested that the Harbour Commission and the federal government build the tunnel. Less than two months later Ottawa pledged $1 million for the construction of a 1,500 foot long, sixty-six-foot-wide auto/streetcar tunnel under the western channel — the project to be carried out as "relief work" as the city struggled in the grips of a world-wide Depression.

A contract was awarded on September 20, 1935 and it appeared as if the city would finally get that illusive "fixed link" to the island. But it was not to be. A change in government resulted in the offer of a million dollars being rescinded. The hole that had been started at the foot of Bathurst Street was backfilled and the project terminated.

Since then the concept of a physical link with the island has been revived numerous times. In the early 1960s a pedestrian tunnel under the Western Channel was suggested, followed a few years later by a Metro Planning Board recommendation that a simple overhead monorail could do the trick. Over the ensuing quarter century nothing has happened so, even though City Council recently approved the construction of a fixed-link, don't hold your breath.

Interestingly, had a 1968 redevelopment project ever gotten off the drawing board the present ruckus would have never arisen. Why? because Harbour City, a community of 50,000 souls living in a sprawling profusion of high rise apartments, would have obliterated not only the Island Airport but the Western Channel as well.

A LASTING TRIBUTE TO OUR FALLEN

November 5, 1995

This year marks the fiftieth anniversary of the end of the Second World War, a war that took the lives of more than 43,000 young men and woman from every part of the Dominion. These soldiers, airmen, sailors, and members of the nation's unsung merchant navy fought and died not for their individual provinces, but for their country, a place they all called Canada.

It's also been seventy-seven years since the end of the First World War and forty-two years since the termination of hostilities in Korea.

Next Saturday, November 11, one of this city's most endearing ceremonies, the Service of Remembrance, will once again take place at the Cenotaph in front of "old" City Hall. This being a special anniversary year, the service will be larger than in recent years. Wreath-laying ceremonies will commence at 10:30 am, with City Hall's trio of bells proclaiming the traditional two minutes of silence at precisely 11 am Mayor Barbara Hall and members of City Council invite all Toronto war veterans to join them at this special Remembrance Day event and at a reception at the nearby Colony Hotel following the service.

* * * * *

Crowds look on as the Earl Haig lays the cornerstone of Toronto's new Cenotaph, July 24, 1925.

The concept of a memorial to honour the city's war dead was first proposed even before hostilities ended at the eleventh hour of the eleventh day of the eleventh month, 1918. But when news of the armistice finally reached Toronto that cold Monday morning the thought of honouring those who had died was put aside as the city erupted into joyous frenzy. A planned Victory Loan parade quickly became a Peace Day (as that first November 11 was dubbed) parade. But the joy turned to sadness as people began to reflect on the 10,000 Torontonians who had made the supreme sacrifice. They would never celebrate the sweet victory.

For the November 11 of 1919, a temporary memorial was constructed in front of the City Hall, and it was here that the city fathers held the first Remembrance Day service.

Four years later, members of City Council began talking about a permanent structure, though there was concern about where this new memorial should be erected. Some suggested Queen's Park, while others thought a place in Allan Gardens would be better. Meanwhile, thousands of returned war veterans urged that the memorial to their dead comrades be placed in front of the City Hall. This time the city fathers listened.

As for the appearance of the proposed memorial, it was decided that an open competition, under the auspices of the Ontario Association of Architects, would be held. Details were finalized and in September, 1924 submissions were invited. Of the several dozen entries received that of William M. Ferguson was selected as the winner.

The Scottish-born and educated Ferguson had emigrated to Canada in 1911. He was invited to join the busy office of architect John Lyle. Lyle's Royal Alexandra Theatre had only been open a short time and

The Great Cenotaph in London, England is a much larger version of Toronto's war memorial.

now the much-in-demand architect was busy on the final plans for the city's massive new Union Station.

After a few years with Lyle's organization, Ferguson joined the firm of Darling and Pearson, Architects, where, according to Ferguson's obituary in the April 18, 1956 *Toronto Telegram*, he helped design Toronto's new general hospital on College Street and was "in charge of designing the dignified Sun Life Building in Montreal."

Next he joined up with Thomas Pomfrey, at which time he decided to submit his idea for Toronto's new war memorial. Ferguson's proposal was a "miniature" version of Sir Edwin Luytens' Great Cenotaph, which had been erected near the intersection of Downing Street and Whitehall in London, England in 1919. And while it would resemble London's Cenotaph, Toronto's would be sculpted from a massive piece of granite from the Canadian Shield.

The cornerstone of Toronto's Cenotaph was laid on July 24, 1925 by the Earl Haig who had served as Commander-in-Chief of the British Forces during the Great War.

On November 11, 1925, seventy years ago next Saturday, a huge crowd gathered in front of Toronto City Hall. Governor General Lord Byng stepped forward from out of that crowd and, pulling on gold cords that secured several large Union Jacks that encircled the monument, unveiled Toronto's new Cenotaph.

Let Honour rule and hatred cease,
So shall our heroes rest in peace.

* * * * *

The fascinating story of Canada's merchant navy, from its glorious beginnings to its unceremonious dissolution, has finally been captured in a new book from Vanwell Publishing. *The Unknown Navy* was written by Robert Halford who joined the merchant marine in 1943 at the age of 20.

WAR MEMORIAL SPARKED (VERBAL) BATTLE

November 12, 1995

Readers will recall that in last week's column I described how the Cenotaph in front of "old" City Hall came into being tracing the impressive memorial's history from the design selection to the official service of dedication that was held on November 11, 1925, exactly seventy years ago yesterday.

It was while searching the files and old newspapers for material related to the Cenotaph that I came across additional information that prompts this second, somewhat unusual story considering the "hallowed" nature of the subject.

When the design put forward by the local architectural firm of Pomfrey and Ferguson was accepted by the appropriate civic officials in early 1925, these same officials also approved (inadvertently as it turned out) the inscription that was to appear on the face of the memorial:

To All Who Served 1914–1918.

When word got out that this wording had been chosen for the new memorial, a major quarrel ensued. Accusations, insinuations, rebuttals, and denials soon began appearing on the front page of the city's daily papers. Toronto's proposed symbol of remembrance was suddenly embroiled in controversy.

Seems that from the very start two years earlier, when Alderman George Shields first suggested that a suitable memorial to honour Torontonians who had died during the Great War be erected in front of the main entrance to City Hall, everyone was under the impression that the memorial would take the form of a cenotaph — a structure that is intended to recognize those who had died, but had been buried in another place. (The word "cenotaph" is derived from the Greek expression for "empty tomb.")

If it was true that the words "To All Who Served 1914–1918" had actually been selected, suddenly every Torontonian who had participated in the war, in any way, was now to be recognized. This arbitrary action by a handful of civic officials was totally unacceptable. The condemnation of their actions was swift.

The inscription "To Our Glorious Dead" appearing on Toronto's impressive Cenotaph was the choice of thousands of returning Great War veterans.

"I'll get no thrill out of passing that monument," declared one of the best-known lieutenant-colonels in Toronto, a man who had a distinguished fighting record. "If it were to the dead, I would feel the awe of it and lift my hat every time I passed, but I cannot subscribe to a monument which is erected to myself as well as the dead."

Another colonel pointed out that regiments passing a memorial to the dead salute it. Unless the words were changed he would not order a salute to the present memorial when marching his men past it.

"We want a memorial to the dead and nothing else will do," said a former soldier. "Imagine laying a wreath on anything else on Armistice Day. The boys who did not live to share the pleasures of home and family and all the world offers us are the ones to whom the city should erect its monument."

A reporter buttonholed former mayor W. W. Hiltz, who was in office when the contentious wording was approved. Hiltz had no explanation for the choice of words, claiming that details concerning the actual inscription were the responsibility of others. He and the selection committee were only interested in the design. After some prodding, Hiltz said he thought that the controversial expression had been incorporated in the architectural renderings. Perhaps that's where the blame should be placed, he suggested.

And even as the debate raged, the craftsmen from McIntosh Granite were desperately trying to get the memorial completed in time for the fast approaching Armistice Day service.

Finally, in an attempt to defuse a situation that was getting more hostile every day, a special meeting of City Council was convened on November 2, at which time it was unanimously agreed to alter the inscription.

As a result, when the Union Jacks encircling the city's new Cenotaph parted seventy years ago yesterday, the one wish of thousands of returned soldiers was recognized with the appearance of the words "To Our Glorious Dead 1914–1918".

BELT LINE LOOPS WERE NO CINCH

August 6, 1995

W hile it may not be a landmark in the usual sense of the word, it's a landmark nevertheless. I'm referring to the former Belt Line steam railway bridge that crosses Yonge Street just south of the Davisville Avenue/Chaplin Crescent intersection. Every day hundreds of cars, trucks, and buses as well as numerous pedestrians pass under it, oblivious to the fact that at one time this structure was an important part of truly innovative public transit service, a service that only lasted a little more than two years.

One of the promoters of this pioneer commuter line was John Thomas Moore, who owned considerable property northeast of the dusty Yonge Street/St. Clair Avenue intersection, an area that was still part of the tranquil countryside surrounding the Toronto of the late 1880s. (A little Toronto trivia, John T. was the Moore of today's Moore Park.)

Yonge Street at Merton looking south to the Belt Line Bridge, 1946.

ON THE TORONTO BELT LINE RAILWAY.

UPPER CANADA COLLEGE.
FROM THE NORTH.

AT YONGE STREET.
LOOKING NORTH.

W.D.B.

Sketch from an 1892 Belt Land Company brochure shows a Belt Line train crossing the Yonge Street bridge while a Metropolitan Railway streetcar glides by underneath. The chimney is adjacent to the streetcar company's powerhouse.

Working in concert with a consortium of prominent city businessmen, Moore was able to convince provincial government officials to give their collective blessing to his new venture, which was to be known as the Toronto Belt Land Corporation. Once the formal charter, dated March 23, 1889, was issued Moore got busy subdividing his holdings and selling off lots for building sites. Before long hundreds of citizens were eagerly buying shares in the new company.

A key element of this new venture would be the introduction of a special commuter rail service (to use modern day terminology) that would allow residents of Moore's suburban community easy access to and from the offices, factories, and theatres in the heart of the city. This service would utilize steam trains pulling neatly appointed passenger cars over a newly constructed rail line that would encircle the city like a belt, an analogy that gave both the company and the commuter service, the Belt Line, their respective names.

In fact, there would be two separate "belts." One would service proposed new developments northwest of the city and would be called the Humber Loop. The second belt, Yonge Loop, would operate through the Don and Spring Valleys (the latter ravine is still visible east of the Moore and Welland Avenue intersection) then move westerly through a yet-unsurveyed part of Mt. Pleasant Cemetery. The line would continue along the north side of the cemetery, over Yonge Street via a bridge (which is still there), continue westerly curving south to the waterfront and back to the station via existing track west of Caledonia Road and Lansdowne Avenue.

Property acquisition was time-consuming and track construction was involved, so the line didn't open until July 30, 1892. At first six round trips in each direction were offered daily on the Yonge Loop with a graded fare, depending on the length of the ride (reminiscent of the TTC "zone-fare" system in effect from 1962–73). A one-way ride from Union Station to the station at the Yonge Street bridge was 8¢.

As innovative as this commuter transit service was, the concept faced failure virtually from the start. Property sales never lived up to the directors' initial expectations and this, combined with an economy that collapsed altogether in 1893, led to a total curtailment of operations over the Belt Line Railway effective November 19, 1894. The service had lasted a mere 842 days.

Most of the rail was torn up during the Great War and while a plan surfaced in 1923 to rebuild the track, electrify the route, and integrate it into the newly established Canadian National Railway's passenger operations nothing further happened. Some freight service over portions of the Belt Line right-of-way continued for a time. Today, the Yonge Loop has been converted by the city into a pleasant "walking park."

Toronto's Link to Lusitania

November 26, 1995

One of the most interesting books amongst the hundreds of new titles to appear on book store shelves around the world this season is the creation of a handful of talented people working right here in Toronto. *Exploring the* Lusitania was written by Dr. Robert Ballard, with the assistance of local author Spencer Dunmore, and published by Madison Press whose offices are on (where else?) Madison Avenue just steps from the city's busy Bloor/Spadina intersection. Ballard, you will recall, "found" another ill-starred ocean liner, *RMS Titanic*, in 1985 documenting that event in an earlier Madison Press best-seller *The Discovery of the* Titanic.

Exploring the Lusitania features a wealth of rare old photographs depicting the once-popular trans-Atlantic ocean liner before she was sent to the bottom by a German torpedo in the spring of 1915 with the loss of nearly 1,200 souls.

Lusitania backs away from New York's Pier 54 to begin her 202 (and last) Atlantic Ocean crossing. May 1, 1915. Courtesy Madison Press.

In addition to dozens of colour photographs taken of the wreck a special feature of this marvelous book is a selection of paintings by talented marine artist Ken Marschall depicting, in life-like detail, the stricken vessel as it appears today resting on the ocean floor off the south coast of Ireland.

* * * * *

News of the glorious liner's sinking was of particular interest to Torontonians since more than 150 of their fellow citizens were on board the huge Cunard liner that had departed the Port of New York on May 1 bound for Liverpool, England.

As friends and relatives awaited the real story of the incident, page after page of the city's various Friday, May 7 newspapers were filled with conflicting reports received by telegraph at the news desks in the hours immediately following the disaster. CNN coverage was decades in the future.

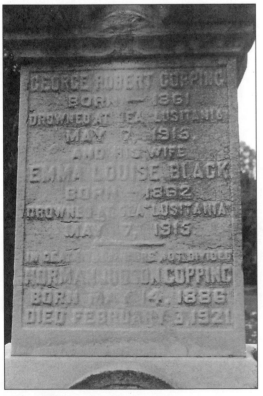

Headstone in Mt. Pleasant Cemetery that reads "George Robert Copping...and his wife Emma Louise...drowned at sea *Lusitania*." The couple lived at 72 South Drive in Rosedale.

As had been the case when the first reports of the *Titanic's* foundering on its maiden voyage in the spring of 1912 were tapped out it appeared as if all *Lusitania's* passengers and crew members were safe. But unlike those initial *Titanic* stories wherein everyone had been rescued by nearby vessels before the ship sank, *Lusitania* had been so close to the Irish coast when the German submarine attacked that it was simply a matter of beaching the giant vessel near the little town of Kinsale. One report even suggested the sinking was caused by the detonation of an "infernal machine" placed on board the ship by foreign agents.

Nevertheless, all were safe. Or so the world thought.

Before long it became clear that those first reports were

wrong and, in fact, the huge vessel had gone down as a result of a well aimed torpedo and the loss of life was going to be horrendous. But now the heart-wrenching question was just who were the lucky ones to survive the sinking. The news was painfully slow in arriving and even the following day's paper had few additional details regarding the names of survivors, or conversely, the victims. Many spent the weekend outside the Cunard Line's Toronto ticketing office run by A.F. Webster at the northeast corner of King and Yonge streets. Through bleary eyes they scanned the ever-lengthening list of Toronto survivors and victims.

By Tuesday the final numbers had been determined. It was obvious that both Canada and this city had been hard hit. Of the 1,265 passengers on board, 322 were Canadian with 155 of that number from Toronto. In all, 175 Canadians had died, a frightful number that included 82 Torontonians. Among the unfortunates were Mr. and Mrs. Alfred Palmer of 65 Vermont Avenue and their three young children. The bodies of these five Torontonians were never found.

Ontario's Very Own "Loveboat"

December 3, 1995

Last week I wrote a column about Dr. Robert Ballard's new publication *Exploring the Lusitania* one of the many new books that I'd love to find under the tree this Christmas. Here are a few more titles, each of which would be a welcome addition to any history buff's library.

While the *Lusitania* may have immensely popular with trans-Atlantic passengers, we here in Toronto had our own favourite, the passenger steamer *Cayuga*, which for half-a-century carried hundreds of thousands of passengers between the Queen City and the Niagara River ports of Niagara-on-the-Lake and Queenston. *Memories of* Cayuga, *Ontario's Love Boat* has just been published by Scarborough author Carol Lidgold. The soft-cover book contains a collection of stories written by people who continue to cherish fond memories of the popular steamer that made its last crossing in 1957 and was sold for scrap in 1961. The book is available for $16.95 (tax and postage included) from Carol M. Lidgold Services, Box 11041, 97 Guildwood Parkway, Scarborough, Ontario M1E 5G5.

And while we're on the Niagara River I mustn't forget to mention William Leonard Hunt, who didn't just sail on it — he walked across it on a rope. The fascinating story of this showman (some called him "the Canadian Blondin"), inventor, explorer, and entrepreneur is recounted in Shane Peacock's new book *The Great Farini* (Viking-Penguin, $29.99). Of special interest to me was Hunt's involvement with Frederick Knapp's revolutionary "roller boat" that still languishes beneath tons of landfill near the foot of Parliament Street.

Moving to a river that's closer to home, Eleanor Darke's *A Mill Should Be Built Thereon* recounts the history of the various mills that operated on the Don River where traffic on the busy Don Valley Parkway now roars over Pottery Road. (Natural Heritage Books, $16.95). Mary Campbell and Barbara Myrvold have authored a new fifty-six-page book, *A Walking Tour of Kew Beach*, which features descriptions and photos of twenty-four Kew Beach sites. It's available from the Toronto Public Library's Beaches, Main, and Northern branches for $8 (plus GST) or by mail. Call 416-393-7535 for further details.

And while we're in the Beach area (to use the original term for this part of town) the Save Our Station people have produced not a book, but a

Niagara Navigation Coy.'s Steamer "Cayuga"

The popular Lake Ontario passenger steamer *Cayuga*, Ontario's own "love boat," is seen steaming up the Niagara River in this c.1910 postcard view.

sweatshirt featuring the likeness of the historic Leuty Lifesaving Station. A great gift for either a Beacher or a son of a Beacher. All proceeds are earmarked for the ongoing preservation and maintenance of this Beach landmark. Available at Randall's Stationery, 964 Kingston Road, and other Beach locations. Call 690-1154 for more info.

Now, to sweeten things up a bit, how about Llewellyn Smith's *The House That Jam Built* (Baby Boomer Press, $19.95) in which the author traces eight generations of Smiths beginning with Silas, who emigrated to the Niagara Peninsula during the American War of Independence. Then there was the most famous of the Smiths, young Ernest Disraeli, who in 1882 established the famous E. D. Smith company. More than a century later this family-owned Canadian business continues to produce some of the world's best jams, jellies, and other food products at its Winona, Ontario and Byhalia, Mississippi plants.

For aviation buffs *Spitfire: The Canadians* by Robert Bracken (Boston Mills Press/Stoddart, $40) features personal memories and stories written by the Canadian pilots and ground crew who flew and serviced the most famous fighter aircraft of the Second World War. The book features vintage photos taken by the various contributors as well as forty colour profiles of the "Spit" created by talented aviation artist Ron Lowry.

A recent arrival in stores is Marilyn Litvak's book on Toronto architect *Edward James Lennox* (Dundurn Press, $19.99). Lennox is best known for his Toronto City Hall and Court House (now "old" City Hall), Casa Loma, and the King Edward Hotel, but Lennox did much, much more. His life and times are skillfully documented with lots of photos in Marilyn's new book.

"DING, DING, DING" GO THE TROLLEYS

December 10, 1995

A t a recent Toronto Transit Commission meeting a proposal to retire the last seventeen Presidents' Conference Committee Streamliners (to give the vehicle it's official designation) from the TTC's roster of streetcars received approval. This action was taken as a result of decreased TTC ridership, a surplus of modern CLRV and ALRV streetcars, and a much-diminished operating budget that makes the elimination of the familiar PCC car preferable, in financial terms, to the expensive alternative of mothballing the dwindling fleet. The Commission estimates that the removal of the remaining PCCs will result in an annual savings of $150,000.

Thankfully, two of the cars, #4500 and #4549, which were rebuilt in 1986 to their "like new" 1951 appearance will be retained for special service so the once omni-present PCC will not vanish totally from city streets.

* * * * *

The first of Toronto's new PCCs (purchase price $21,500 per car!) are introduced at a special ceremony at Wychwood and St. Clair avenues, September 23, 1938.

#4063 split a switch on Lansdowne Avenue on January 20, 1947 and crashed into the carhouse wall. Its back broken, the car became the first PCC to be "taken off strength."

The streetcar on the left is one of 140 Toronto PCCs sold to the Alexandria, Egypt transit authority in 1966–67. Wonder if any are still operating?

Introduced to Torontonians in 1938, the PCC car was the culmination of years of research that led to the creation of what could truly be called "the state of the art" in street railway technology, although I'm sure those precise words weren't in vogue back then. The new PCC car eliminated all that was bad with the Commission's ancient wooden ex-Toronto Railway Company streetcars, and was a major improvement over the steel "Peter Witt" cars that had been introduced in 1921.

As the years went by the PCC fleet, which at one point numbered 750 vehicles, continued to rack up hundreds of thousands of miles as they faithfully carried passengers to and from places of work or play. Every once in a while a plan would surface advocating the removal of streetcars from city streets, but the Streamliners kept rolling along. On a couple of occasions aging PCCs were even given new leases on life as a result of major rebuilding programs, the most recent carried out just a few years ago.

But now it looks like it's really the end of the line for these icons of our city's landscape. Heritage frequently takes a hit when money gets tight.

IN THE MOOD TO REMEMBER MILLER

December 17, 1995

The article in the December 26, 1944 edition of the *Evening Telegram* newspaper wasn't very detailed. In fact, given the significance of the event, its location on a page well back in the paper is even more surprising. The item simply stated that "Major Glenn Miller, noted dance band leader, now serving with the U. S. Army Air Forces, has been missing in action since December 15. He entered the service about 2 years ago to conduct service bands and has been in England about a year."

That's it. No screaming headline as one would expect following the disappearance of a man who was at the time leader of what was arguably the world's most popular dance band. Perhaps the brevity of the report was a result of the wartime censors stepping in.

More than half-a-century has passed since that *Telegram* article ran. Over the years the real story on how Miller died is still subject to speculation. One version had his plane, en route to Paris, France, shot down while another

Artist Keith Hill's depiction of Glenn Miller's Canadian-built aircraft departing Turnwood Farm airfield shortly before the band leader's disappearance, December 15, 1944.

suggests that the plane was hit by a bomb dropped by a Royal Air Force *Lancaster* getting rid of its load after returning from an aborted raid into Germany. Some researchers have even proposed a theory that the aircraft veered off course soon after take-off and subsequently crashed in the impenetrable Lincolnshire fens.

Most believe, however, that the single-engine, wood-and-canvas plane in which Miller was a passenger simply "iced up" and plummeted into the English Channel killing all three on board.

At the time of his disappearance Miller's distinctive music was as popular here in Canada as it was in the States or overseas, but unfortunately for his Canadian fans Miller and his band had seldom traveled north of the border. In fact the group had performed only once here in Toronto. The show was on January 23, 1942 and the seventeen-piece band, one of the largest to ever perform in the city, along with songstress Marion Hutton, tenor Roy Eberle, and the Modernaires, performed at the old Arena on Mutual Street. So popular was the Miller event scalpers were able to get as much as $5 for some of the 5,000 dollar-and-a-half tickets. Obviously, the art of scalping is nothing new.

There's no doubt that this visit to Canada was a happy one for Miller the show being a complete sell-out. Unfortunately for Glenn his next association with our country was far less pleasant, for in a strange twist of fate the aircraft in which he was to be a reluctant passenger that cold December day in 1944 was C-64 *Norseman*, a product of the Noorduyn company of Montreal, Quebec. The pilot that day was an ex-RCAF officer.

The control tower at Twinwood Farm as it looks today. An American entrepreneur has talked about moving the building brick by brick to a museum in the States.

During a recent visit to England my wife and I visited the site of the airfield from which Major Miller departed at 13:55, December 15, 1944. Known as Twinwood Farm airfield and located just north of Bedford, its runways have long since disappeared. However, the outbuildings and control tower are still very much in evidence. It was eerie to stand in the room where Miller had waited for his flight. One could almost hear *Norseman* 470285 approaching through the fog and icy drizzle. "You know, he was reluctant to go," our guide advised. "People on duty that day later remarked that it was as if Miller knew something bad was going to happen."

After our visit I chatted with aviation artist Keith Hill, who lives not far from the airfield and has captured Miller's departure from Twinwood Farm in a special commemorative painting. Drop me a line c/o the *Sunday Sun* if you'd like to know more about obtaining a print of Keith's work.

Following the appearance of this article I received a number of requests for information on how to order a copy of Keith Hill's eerie painting of Miller's plane leaving the Twinwood airfield. Here is the pertinent information. Address letters to the artist c/o 24 St. Peter's Avenue, Rushden, Northants, England NN10 6XW.

The Glenn Miller Orchestra (with popular Tex Beneke conducting) appeared at Toronto's Royal York Hotel June 14, 1946, less than six months after Glenn's disappearance. Note that tickets were $2!!

JOHNNY MADE CHRISTMAS A MAGICAL TIME FOR US KIDS

December 24, 1995

P age 6 columnist Gary Dunford and I were chatting a few days ago about the variety of new books that always seem to hit the bookstores just in time for Christmas. "I, too have a new book" I piped up. The gentleman that he is, Gary kindly offered to run a contest in his column awarding copies of my new *Toronto Sketches 4: The Way We Were* (there's the plug) to the best "memories of Christmases past" submitted by his readers.

As we chatted I got to reminiscing about what I could remember about Christmases gone by. My eyes glazed over and suddenly I was standing in a place called Toyland up on the fifth floor of the now-demolished Eaton's main store at Yonge and Queen streets.

Each Christmas, starting when I was 5 or 6, my mother, younger brother and I would walk up Bathurst Street from our third-floor flat at #758 to the Bloor Street corner, board an eastbound streetcar (like those they just retired), take it as far as Yonge Street, change to a Yonge car (they were bigger, older, had stoves, and were operated by a trio of guys in black TTC uniforms, two in the front car, the other back in the trailer), and head downtown.

After what seemed like an eternity slugging through the bunched up Yonge Street traffic we finally entered the big Eaton's store. Yuch, look at all the clothing stuff. Come on, what we want's way upstairs.

Not so fast! First came the compulsory stop to see my Aunt Peg who worked in the "Beddings and Linen" department on the second floor. Another delay. Here we'd be stripped of our snow boots, hats, mittens, snowsuit, etc., etc. Were winters really that much colder back then?

Back on the elevator and an unbelievably slow climb skyward. Come on make this thing go faster. Please, please don't push any of those other buttons. Finally the doors parted and there it was, a wonderland called Toyland. You know, I can still remember riding the shiny black miniature CN train through Santa's Grotto, although I never did find out what a Grotto was. I can also remember sitting on the ice-cold hardwood floor trying out every mechanical toy I could get my hands on and wishing Santa would bring me one of every Dinky toy ever made and a whole bunch of Meccano stuff while he was at it.

Oh yes, there was the mandatory visit with Santa. After all, it was his place.

Johnny Giordmaine, Eaton's amazing Toyland magician.

Now I probably shouldn't divulge this, especially this close to the big day, but the person I really looked forward to seeing in that special place wasn't Santa at all. It was the diminutive Toyland magician, a fellow whose name I didn't learn until years later. We'd watch him for what seemed like hours as he thrilled his audience with his feats of legerdemain. In fact, one time he even pulled a quarter out of my ear.

As I returned to the real world, it became apparent that as captivated as I had been by the little man in Toyland those many years ago, I really didn't know anything about him. I was going to rectify that. A quick look in the clipping files in the *Sun* library and there he was.

John Giordmaine was born in Malta at the end of the last century, one of twelve children. While working as a telephone repair man in a local shipyard, Johnny won a bursary that allowed him to travel. He discovered Toronto and before long moved here.

While working as an electrician at the Swift meat packing plant on St. Clair West, Johnny began studying magic by mail order, quickly absorbing the entire six-volume course offered by the famous Tarbell of Chicago. He got a part-time job in a novelty shop located in the now-demolished Yonge Street Arcade. Here Johnny met the world's best magicians who, while in Toronto to perform at one of the city's many burlesque and vaudeville houses, would stop by the store. Johnny's talents were so profound that within three years he had become the T. Eaton Company's full time-magician.

During Johnny's long and successful career he amazed thousands all over the world. Among his fans were Prime Minister Mackenzie King, Governor General Viscount Alexander, and Eleanor Roosevelt, wife of the American president. Johnny also appeared on the Captain Kangaroo and Ed Sullivan Television shows. Many declared that he was the best magician they had ever seen. But Johnny loved his place behind Eaton's Toyland magic counter most.

On his seventy-third birthday, John was quoted as saying that his chosen audience was children. "Their gasps of amazement and innocent laughter are two of the greatest rewards in life." Christmas, 1973 was Johnny Giordmaine's last. He died less than a month later. I wish I had known him better.

To all *Sun* readers, Merry Christmas
from my wife Yarmila and me.

How We Rang in 1946

December 31, 1995

There was little doubt that the 1945 version of New Year's Eve was going be an extra-special one for Canadians. For the past six years the country had been focussing all of its efforts on winning a world war, a war that would take the lives of nearly 43,000 Canadians. During those six long years there was precious little to celebrate as each old year turned into a new.

But now, with victory in both the European and Asian theatres of war finally realized, 1945's New Year's Eve celebrations would be different!

For those planning a night on the town, news reports warned that revellers should be prepared to pay a cover charge of as much as $8 to $10 a couple (refreshments and taxes extra) to ring in the new year at the more popular restaurants and clubs. Those on a tighter budget could expect to pay $6 a couple (refreshments and taxes included) to participate in the New Year's Eve Dance Party festivities at the Club Queensway (later renamed the Palace Pier) on the west side of the Humber River south of Lakeshore Road in Etobicoke Township.

The same price held at the Piccadilly Hotel, 106 King Street West, where Frank Busseri and his Orchestra (I wonder if he was related to the Frank Busseri of the Four Lads?) were to perform. If $6 was still too stiff, Paul Firman and his Orchestra offered their brand of "so-danceable-music" on two floors of the Masonic Temple at Yonge and Davenport. (The Temple's still there, opposite Canadian Tire.) The $2.50 per person admission charge included dancing, dining, hats, and horns. Still too much money? For a buck-and-a-half you could dance the night away to the music of Ellis McLintock and his Orchestra at Maple Leaf Gardens. Across Yonge Street at the Foresters' Hall, 22 College Street, George Wade and His Corn Huskers would be playing, as the ad read, "the latest in modern dancing and by far the best in old time." (What! No line dancing?)

Rather skate the new year in? The Strathcona Rollerdrome at 586 Christie Street offered a special New Year's Eve Roller Skating Carnival from 9:30 pm until 2 am featuring Gladys McKay at the organ. Admission, 50¢. Icelandia at 1941 Yonge Street (it's now a Speedy Muffler) offered an evening of "strictly supervised" ice skating.

How 'bout taking in a movie? *Frontier Gal* starring Vancouver's own Yvonne De Carlo was the Uptown Theatre's New Year's Eve presentation while at the Imperial (now Pantages) the whole family could be enthralled by the new Disney feature-length movie *Wonderful Adventures of Pinocchio*.

Though peace had returned Torontonians still had concerns as they welcomed in 1946. Concerns such as would their hockey team ever get better. So far the Leafs had only won seven out of twenty-four games and were fifth in the six-team league. One bright spot was Gaye Stewart, the team's top scorer with nineteen goals, the same as the league leading Max Bentley of the Chicago Black Hawks. The Leafs would finish the year in fifth with Stewart scoring a total of thirty-seven goals. In 1947 Bentley joined the Leaf team.

Fifty years ago today many citizens were still undecided as to how they'd vote the next day. (Back then municipal elections were held on New Year's Day.) Mayor Robert Saunders was in by acclamation, but just who would fill positions as controllers and aldermen was still an uncertainty. Plus there were three important questions to answer on that 1946 ballot: should the TTC build a subway under Yonge Street? Should the city build the Clifton Road Extension (it's now known as the Mt. Pleasant Road Extension)? And should a new traffic artery be built in the Don Valley? (As it turned out, the trio received overwhelming approval.)

And while on the subject of traffic, things were bound to get even worse now that the government was set to end tire rationing on January 1, 1946. On-street parking in downtown Toronto was already a serious problem. Plans were afoot to build an underground parking lot beneath land being held for a new municipal building. Nearly twenty years went by before that lot, and the new city hall, opened.

Happy New Year!!

TODAY
A WHIRLWIND WORLD OF ADVENTURE and FUN

You thrill...amazed and almost unbelieving...as it unfolds before your astonished eyes...in stunning color, merry with song...and so exciting, you'll want to see it twice!

Walt Disney's
WONDERFUL ADVENTURES OF Pinocchio

FULL-LENGTH FEATURE IN TECHNICOLOR

YOU'LL SEE THEM ALL plus 100 others!

On the same program
STAR IN THE NIGHT
The featurette that has been mentioned as the Academy Award winner for this year

IMPERIAL
A FAMOUS PLAYERS THEATRE

Toronto Evening Telegram ad for the new Walt Disney film *Wonderful Adventures of Pinocchio* at the Imperial Theatre on Yonge Street.

MODEL GUIDE TO THE PAST

January 7, 1996

In 1978 one of Toronto's most historic buildings was ravaged by fire. Once the conflagration was extinguished, it appeared as if the wreckers would have to be called in to level yet another city landmark.

Fortunately, however, Sheldon and Judy Godfrey came to the rescue and Toronto's First Post Office was given a new lease on life, as were the adjacent Bank of Upper Canada and De La Salle buildings.

Co-incident with the rebirth of these important structures, a new volunteer organization was established to help guide the future of this new attraction. In addition, the Town of York Historical Society was charged with the task of drawing the public's attention to what is, arguably, the most historic part of the city. To that end the society undertook a number of interesting projects one of which was the construction of a large three-

The Bank of Upper Canada (erected 1825–27) at the northeast corner of Adelaide and George streets with the 1871 De La Salle school additions to the right. Toronto's First Post Office is out of the view to the extreme right.

dimensional scale model of Toronto as the young city would have looked in 1837, just four years after the old post office building was erected. The model was unveiled in the fall of 1992, but until now hasn't had anything in written form to help visitors identify the various structures and landscape features that appear on the model.

That's now been rectified thanks to the recent publication by the society of a well-researched spiral-bound book that will also serve as a handy walking tour guide of the Town of York (if and when it ever warms up again).

Toronto 1837: A Model City was co-written by Jennifer Parsons and Kevin Lilliman and is available for a very reasonable $12.95 (plus GST) at Toronto's First Post Office, 260 Adelaide Street East (between Jarvis and Sherbourne streets) or by phone (416-865-1833).

* * * * *

While the sixty illustrations in the book are period sketches, those accompanying this column are photographs taken when photography was still in its infancy.

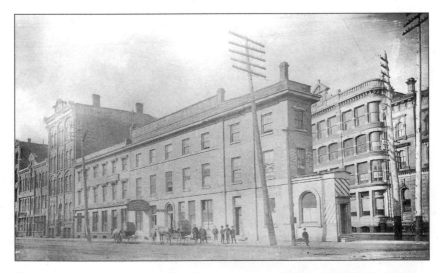

Known colloquially as the "coffin block" (because of its resemblance to a giant casket) this c.1830 landmark stood at the Wellington, Front, and Church intersection until its demolition in the early 1890s. The "Flatiron Building" now stands on the site, and has for more than a century.

WINGING IT INTO AVIATION HISTORY

January 21, 1996

More than eighty years ago, a Canadian developed an aircraft — the Bonisteel monoplane — that some felt would revolutionize the aviation industry worldwide.

Today, many aviation historians recognize Bonisteel's brave attempt as the first aircraft to be built, start to finish, here in Canada.

Ernest Dickens Bonisteel was born in Belleville, Ontario in 1894. In the early teens Toronto city directories list the young man, by then a practicing architect, as a resident of 15 Close Avenue in the Parkdale area of the city. In those far-off days the tree-lined north-south streets in that quiet neighbourhood all began at the water's edge. The construction of Lake Shore Boulevard in the 20s and the Gardiner Expressway thirty years later have obliterated any trace of the inventor's house.

In fact, all we really have to remind us of this visionary inventor are a few contemporary newspaper reports, an article by Les Wilkinson in the Canadian Aviation Historical Society's Journal, and a few rare old snapshots of the man and his machine.

One of those old newspaper accounts describes in some detail the project that had kept young Bonisteel busy while war was raging in far away Europe. The report indicated that authorities were more interested in seeing the young inventor perfect his two-seat "flying boat" rather than shipping him off to Europe to join the hundreds of thousands of young Canadians at the front.

Authorities were placing great emphasis on the flying machines as fundamental to a quick Allied victory.

As for the young inventor, not only did he have the skills of an architect, he had also gained some experience with the Polson Iron Works people, a company that had constructed several of the Toronto Island ferry boats (including *Trillium*). That fact probably accounts for Bonisteel's desire to create an airplane of the "flying boat" variety.

And that's exactly what he did, although it's not known whether the actual assembly of his craft was done at the Close Avenue location or in the large tent he had erected under the old steel bridge that connected Lakeshore Road with Queen, King, and Roncesvalles at Sunnyside. The tent

Volunteer workers carry out restoration work on the CF-100 positioned on a pedestal in Wildwood Park, Derry Road, Malton.

protected his airplane from the elements, curious passersby, and perhaps even spies.

It is also unclear as to whether the twin-seat, single-wing airplane (both somewhat revolutionary features) ever actually flew.

A very rare photo of the Bonisteel monoplane with the Sunnyside bridge and "factory" tent in the background.

Reminiscing years later, some of Bonisteel's contemporaries recalled seeing the machine airborne but couldn't recall whether it was a lengthy flight or one of the Howard Hughes *Spruce Goose* variety that is in the air long enough to say it was in the air. There's also some speculation that it was the lack of an adequate engine that was to doom the craft to oblivion.

We do know that Lieutenant Bonisteel abandoned the project and went oversees in 1916.

A few years later all that was left of the Bonisteel monoplane — a broken rudder emblazoned with a painted Union Jack, a control wheel, and a few wing and fuselage fragments — were collected with a view to putting the artifacts on display in the Yonge Street offices of the Aero Club. Like Bonisteel's dream, these plans were eventually abandoned.

While on the subject of aviation firsts, last Friday marked the forty-sixth anniversary of the preliminary flight of the CF-100, the first Canadian-designed and built jet fighter. This aircraft was designed by the talented staff at the Malton, Ontario factory of AVRO Canada. Not far from the AVRO factory one of the few remaining CF-100s (a total of 692 were built) rests proudly on a pedestal in Wildwood Park. This past summer #18619 underwent extensive restorative work thanks to the members of the Aerospace Heritage Foundation of Canada and several corporate sponsors. Details concerning Foundation membership can be obtained by contacting the AHFC at P.O. Box 246, Etobicoke "D", Etobicoke M9A 4X2.

FALLING VICTIM TO THE DEADLY FLU BUG

January 28, 1996

As much we all love Canadian winters, it's unfortunate that many miss the splendours of the season suffering from the effects of the common cold or recuperating from the more serious symptoms of influenza, an ailment better known as simply the "flu." And yet as devoted as members of the medical research fraternity are, and in spite of the millions of dollars spent annually seeking cures each year, we're warned that the coming year's strain of flu bug could be worse than any yet experienced, some even suggesting that it is quite possible that the next outbreak could be worse even than the dreadful "Spanish flu" epidemic that struck world-wide in 1918–19. It has been estimated that between 25 and 50 million flu victims succumbed world-wide to the ravages of the affliction (which was so-named because the first epidemic to reach the still sparsely populated North American continent centuries before had supposedly been carried across the Atlantic by a native of Valencia, Spain).

More exact figures were impossible to estimate since the vast majority of deaths occurred in countries where medical treatment was primitive. The decimation of crowded cities in China and India was unfortunate, but understandable considering the existing sanitation standards.

Here in Canada we were not immune to the rapidly spreading disease. More than 50,000 Canadians died either directly from the influenza virus (though at the time neither the virus connection or penicillin had been discovered) or as a result of pneumonia that assailed the weakened patient. Those afflicted suffered for two or three days then either recovered or died. It was that simple ... and swift.

Amazingly, the total number of Canadians who died during the epidemic was only 10,000 fewer than the total number of Canadians killed during the four years of the Great War, which was slowly winding down. That number also approximated the total number of Canadians who died during the entire six years of the Second World War.

Here in Toronto (with its population of less than half-a-million) the first reported flu death was that of a twelve-year-old who, before leaving for school, complained of a cold. But because most family members were also "under the weather," no remedial action was taken. That was Wednesday. By Thursday her symptoms had worsened and she was taken to hospital. On Saturday, the youngster was dead.

Throughout October, 1918 more and more cases of influenza were reported, and before long school hallways were virtually empty as both students and teachers became victims. And as the schools emptied hospital wards began to fill, with many of the patients stricken nurses and doctors. One thing was for sure, the flu wasn't particular about its victims.

Soon twenty deaths a day wasn't an unusual occurrence. People were urged to wear gauze masks and to refrain from kissing. Some even suggested that eating onions could ward off germs.

But patients in the big city hospitals weren't the only ones suffering. Scattered around Toronto were a number of military hospitals where returning soldiers were recuperating from illness or war wounds. It was in these cramped quarters that many flu victims could be found. City and provincial officials got into shouting matches with military personnel, who seemed to be oblivious to the problem. The army knew best and the municipality was told in no uncertain terms to mind its own business. Eventually cooler heads prevailed and soon the unfortunates in draughty, unheated, makeshift hospital wards were being removed to more comfortable locations.

The former General Hospital on Gerrard Street East was reactivated as a military hospital during the Great War. Many of its patients were to succumb to the Spanish flu.

One building that had been pressed into service was the rambling old Toronto General Hospital on the north side of Gerrard Street just west of the Don River. Erected nearly seventy years earlier in a part of the city that was still countryside, the old hospital buildings had been abandoned when the modern new General Hospital opened on College Street in 1913. Now it was being used as the Base Hospital.

The worst day was October 23, 1918 when a total of eighty-seven people succumbed to either flu or pneumonia. Deaths here and in city hospitals became so frequent that officials, for the first time in the city's history, ordered that burials be carried out on Sundays.

As October came to an end, so too did the incidence of new influenza cases, by which time more than 1,600 Torontonians had become victims.

The flu scare was already just a memory when carefree crowds gathered on November 11 to welcome the news that the "war to end all wars" was over.

Getting a Leg up on "N-Day" Invasion

February 4, 1996

With February 14 a little more than a week away, I wonder if anyone still buys nylon stockings to give as Valentine's Day gifts? Well, exactly fifty years ago this weekend word was going around that, after a long absence due to war restrictions, nylon stockings would soon be back in the stores. Unfortunately, their return missed Valentine's Day, 1946 by five days. Nevertheless, when February 19 finally arrived so too did the nylons, and for clerks in ladies' clothing stores around town that day would turn out to be a day like no other in living memory.

Nylon (or more precisely a class of thermoplastic polyamide synthesized by the interaction of dicarboxylic acid with a diamine — and they said a

The Reitman's store on the west side of Yonge just north of Queen was especially busy on February 19, 1946 when nylons again became available. Woolworth's (store with awning at the Yonge-Queen corner, now the site of the new Tower record store) and Kresge's had nylons as well, but many forgot that the chain stores had also received supplies. Here the lineups were smaller.

A Limited Quantity of

NYLON
HOSIERY

will be available at

Northway's

TUESDAY, FEBRUARY 19th

We have decided upon the following method of distribution as the fairest way to serve our customers:

1 — NYLON Hosiery will be located ACCORDING TO SIZE at various sections of the Main Floor. The entire Main Floor will be used if necessary.

2 — Customers on entering the store will FIRST OBTAIN A NUMBERED CARD for the size they require.

3 — CUSTOMERS will then proceed to their size section where they will be served according to their card number. Payment will be made at this point.

4 — SALES WILL BE LIMITED to one pair to each customer.

5 — We will be unable to accept orders by telephone or mail until further notice.

We realize we will not have a sufficient supply to serve all our customers on this day, but further shipments of NYLON Hosiery will be received in the near future.

This method of distribution will also be used in the Northway Stores in
HAMILTON, CHATHAM, BRANTFORD, STRATFORD and ORILLIA

JOHN NORTHWAY AND SON LIMITED — 240 Yonge Street, Toronto

Advertisement announcing the return of nylons to Northway's.

chemistry education was wasted on me) was first produced in the research laboratories of the E. I. du Pont de Nemours organization and patented in early 1937. The new discovery was first used, commercially, to make toothbrush bristles. Nylon yarn wasn't produced until late 1939, with the first nylon stockings appearing in stores south of the border on May 15, 1940. Following the States' entry into the war the unique characteristics of nylon resulted in its removal from consumer products in all the allied countries as production was focussed on war-related items, especially parachute cord and fabric.

With the cessation of hostilities in 1945, nylon, in various forms and in various products, was again headed for store shelves. By far the most eagerly awaited of all the consumer goods using nylon were ladies stockings. The government announced that between the time the war ended and the end of 1945 exactly 2,212,516 pairs of nylons had been manufactured in the various hosiery mills across the country. These same officials promised that Torontonians would get their quota commencing on what was termed "N-Day" ("D-Day," "V-E Day," and "V-J Day" having already passed into history).

When February 19, 1946 finally arrived the pandemonium that erupted in the vicinity of the various department and ladies' wear stores where the treasured nylons were back in stock could only be compared to the ruckus that broke out all over the city on V-E Day. At store opening time lineups had as many as 3,000 people waiting — and not all were women. One of the earliest arrivals at the Northway store on Yonge Street (demolished to make way for the Eaton Centre) was an air force man who, when asked why he wanted the nylons, replied that he was going to trade them for a good home-cooked meal.

As nearly perfect as the new nylon stockings were supposed to be, an interesting comment was offered by one female purchaser at an Evangeline store (where the 45- and 49-gauge nylons were $1.75 a pair, 51-gauge, $1.95). As it was exceedingly cold that February day a half century ago (ten degrees above zero using the old Fahrenheit scale) she decided under these conditions the old rayon stockings were better because they were warmer. I guess there's no pleasing everybody.

ROLLING OUT THE LATEST MODELS

February 11, 1996

Since the very early years of this century, car shows of one sort or another have been part of this city's history. In fact, it's a matter of record that the city's first auto show was held just six years after Dr. Perry Doolittle of 419 Sherbourne Street purchased his "horseless carriage" from Hamiltonian John Moodie, thus becoming the first Torontonian to own a gasoline-powered automobile.

The car that Doolittle bought in 1898 was a second-hand one-cylinder Winton Phaeton that Moodie had acquired new for $1,000 from its creator Alexander Winton, a one-time Cleveland, Ohio bicycle builder. (An interesting sidelight to the Moodie deal was that its purchase was the easy part of the deal. Getting the mechanized contraption across the border into Canada was tougher. Customs officials, listing the auto as a "carriage,"

The US-built Chalmers automobile was displayed in the Transportation Building at the 1911 CNE. This car, which was sold by Eaton's, would become history just a dozen years later.

assessed a thirty-five percent duty on it. Moodie fought the bureaucracy and had the vehicle reclassified as a "locomotive," a product taxable at only twenty-five percent.)

It wasn't long after Dr. Doolittle began puttering around town that other locals began trading in their horses for other forms of horsepower. Sir John Eaton, for instance, had a Stanley steamer while his cousin R.Y. Eaton and other local business tycoons such as George Gooderham, Frank Baillie, Mark Irish, and Colonel Bickford opted for autos with internal-combustion gasoline engines.

On April 23, 1904 the Canada Cycle and Motor Company, a well-known local bicycle manufacturing concern, announced that during "Horse Show Week" it would host Toronto's *first* Automobile Show in the company's premises at the northeast corner of Bay and Temperance streets, a location dubbed by the company for that week at least, "Automobile Corner." Entrance to the show, where a number of different makes sold by CCM were on display, was by invitation only. In the bicycle business since 1896, CCM could see a new source of business through the sale of automobiles. In later years the company would actually enter the car manufacturing business, turning out the Ivanhoe electric car and the Russell gasoline-powered cars, the latter reputed to be the first successful all-Canadian car.

By 1909 interest in automobiles had increased to such an extent that not one, but two separate auto shows were held. The first, identified as the Automobile and Motor Boat Show, took place at the Granite Club rink, 513 Church Street. It hadn't been over for a week when "the Real Big Automobile Show" got underway at the Mutual Street Arena (which years later would be remodelled and open as The Terrace curling rink). Both shows featured American, French, and British built cars.

As the years went by the city hosted numerous car shows with many of those held in the now-demolished University Avenue Armouries. Several shows were held on the sixth floor of the newly constructed Simpson store addition at Richmond and Bay streets. (Cars were hoisted up the outside of the building and pushed in through modified window openings.) Ford even introduced its 1932 lineup at Eaton's new College Street store.

And while a few new autos were displayed under tents at the Exhibition in the early years of the century (including Toronto inventor/patent lawyer Frederick Fetherstonhaugh's revolutionary electric car), it wasn't until 1908 that fair officials finally recognized the impact new cars were having on people and ordered that plans be prepared for a special automobile (and, just to be safe, carriage) exhibit hall. The Transportation Building (by then known as the Spanish Pavilion) burned to the ground in 1974.

In 1929 the present Automobile Building was dedicated by provincial premier Howard Ferguson, who described the million-dollar structure as "a timely tribute to the automotive industry." For years the new cars were the main attraction of the annual fair. When the CNE decided to open the fair in mid-August, well in advance of the new car introduction dates, auto displays vanished from the Exhibition.

The twenty-third annual Canadian International Auto Show will be held at the Metro Toronto Convention Centre and SkyDome from February 15–25, 1996.

*　*　*　*　*

In a recent article about Glenn Miller I reproduced a painting done by artist Keith Hill depicting the big band leader's fateful departure from Twynwood Farm near Bedford in England, December 15, 1944. In response to numerous requests, information about purchasing a print of that painting can be obtained by writing the artist at 24 St. Peter's Avenue, Rushden, Northants, England NN10 6XW.

YONGE AT HEART

February 18, 1996

I t was two hundred years ago today, February 18, 1796, that John Graves Simcoe, lieutenant-governor of the recently created Province of Upper Canada (renamed Ontario in 1867), eagerly awaited word on the status of a new road he had ordered blazed through the dense forest surrounding the small settlement of York. The trail was stretch northward exactly thirty-four miles and fifty-three chains (one chain = sixty-six feet) to the "Pine Fort" (subsequently renamed Holland Landing after the surveyor-general Samuel Holland). As far as the governor was concerned, the necessity of a road leading to and from the small naval shipyard which he had established in 1793 at a place the native people called Toronto (but which the governor had quickly renamed York in recognition of King George III's twenty-nine-year-old son Frederick the Duke of York) was disturbingly obvious. The sting of Britain's recent defeat during the Revolutionary War (or War of Independence depending on whose side you were on) was still fresh in the governor's

Postcard view showing the Yonge Street crossing of the Don River at the turn-of-the-century. Note that the Scottish-produced card got the spelling of "Hogg's" incorrect (as many still do).

A LITTLE BIT ABOUT SIR GEORGE
YONGE

Sir George Yonge was born in England in 1731, educated at Eton and Leipzig, and elected to parliament as the member for Honiton, Devonshire in 1754. Honiton was the location of John Graves Simcoe's Wolford Lodge estate, so it was inevitable that the two would meet frequently. In July, 1782 Yonge was appointed secretary of state for war in the cabinet of King George III, serving until July, 1794 (except for the brief period April–November, 1783). Sir George (he was knighted in 1788) was then asked to serve as master of the mint — a position he held until February, 1799. He was then appointed governor of the Cape of Good Hope. Sir George died on September 25, 1812 and is buried in a vault at the parish church of St. Andrew, Colyton, Devon. Sir George's "Great House" in Colyton is still occupied as a residence.

Interestingly, one of Sir George's favourite pastimes was the study of Roman road building. On numerous occasions, he would be called on to interpret ancient ruins uncovered during late-eighteenth-century construction projects in various parts of the country. With the term "street" derived from the latin term "strata," it's somewhat ironic that this Roman road building expert is remembered today in the name of the world's longest street. And no, Sir George never did visit Canada.

memory. He had been wounded three times and taken prisoner, and even though the war ended in 1881 there was no doubt in his mind that sooner or later American forces would attempt to complete their liberation of the continent by attacking the remaining British possessions — including his prime responsibility, the Province of Upper Canada. And when that time came a road to and from York would enable reinforcements from British military posts located on the upper lakes to come to the rescue.

Plans to build this pioneer thoroughfare, named by Simcoe in honour of his long-time friend Sir George Yonge (see sidebar on this page), were being formulated soon after the governor's arrival at the future site of Metropolitan Toronto. However, with further threats of war and the cancellation of a plan that would have seen the road completed by land speculator William Von Berczy, real work didn't commence until January 4, 1796. On that day thirty members of the Queen's Rangers (see sidebar on page 85), accompanied by surveyor Augustus Jones, set out from York with axe and adze in hand. Forty-three days later they had reached their goal.

On February 20, 1796 Jones attended on the governor in his office at Fort York, advising him that the road had been opened from York to the Pine Fort Landing, Lake Simcoe. Yonge Street was born.

In the two hundred years that have passed the thirty-four mile, fifty-three chain length of pioneer highway has been extended numerous times, the most recent being the completion in 1965 of the 86.7 miles of highway between Atikokan and Fort Frances. The street, either named or with the numerical designation 11 that was assigned by the province in 1925, now stretches a total of 1,178.3 miles (1,896.2 km) terminating at Rainy River, Ontario where the street connects with the bridge into Baudette, Minnesota. Yonge Street, or its alter ego Highway #11 has the distinction of being listed in the Guinness Book as the longest street in the world.

A LITTLE YONGE STREET TRIVIA

• Toll roads, like the new Highway 407 will be, are nothing new. Pioneer travellers on Yonge Street paid tolls as they commuted up and down the street with "pay-as-you-pass" gates at Bloor and at the top of the hill into Hogg's Hollow. Others were located at Thornhill, Elgin mills, Aurora, and Newmarket. Tolls were eliminated in 1896. Or were they?

• The first public transit operator on Yonge Street was Henry Burt Williams who, when he lost out to transit promoters from the United States in 1861, reverted to his other business profession. He was an undertaker.

• The first street railway system in Canada opened on Yonge Street on September 11, 1861. The *Yonge* streetcar operated continuously until March 30, 1954. On that day Canada's first subway opened, replacing the historic *Yonge* streetcar line.

• The last radial car to Lake Simcoe ran on Yonge Street ran on March 15, 1930. The line was reinstated as far as Richmond Hill the following

QUEEN'S RANGERS

First raised as a British scouting force in 1755 by the legendary Robert Rogers, the regiment eventually came under the command of John Graves Simcoe, and was soon given the title "First American Regiment" by King George III. In 1796 members of the Queen's Rangers constructed the first short section of the new Yonge Street. Then, as the York Volunteers, the regiment helped turn back invading Americans at Queenston Heights during the War of 1812. Renamed the Queen's Rangers once again, the regiment defended Toronto during Mackenzie's unsuccessful revolt in 1837. And when the Fenian Brotherhood attacked Canada at Fort Erie in 1866, the regiment, now designated the 12th Battalion York Rangers, helped repulse the invaders. Members of the Rangers went on to serve in the First World War in various battalions. In 1936, the 1st Battalion York Rangers amalgamated with the Queen's Rangers to become the Queen's York Rangers (First American Regiment), and as such were responsible for Canadian territorial defence during the Second World War. In 1947 the regiment became the 25th Armoured Regiment returning to the designation Queen's York Rangers (1st American Regiment) in 1965.

Yonge Street looking north from Front Street, c.1925.

Passengers await a northbound Yonge streetcar at the Richmond Street corner, c.1950.

Yonge Street looking north at the south end of Richmond Hill, 1909.

Yonge Street north to the College/Carlton intersection. c.1915. The jog in the latter two streets was eliminated as a "depression work" in 1931.

July 17. That line terminated on October 10, 1948, a victim of electricity shortages that plagued the province following the end of the Second World War.

• Aerial transportation came to Yonge Street more than seventy years ago when a couple of small airfields opened adjacent to the street. The first, on the site of the present North York City Hall, opened in 1927. The other airfield opened on the east side of Yonge, just north of today's Bishop Avenue, the following year.

• Housing subdivisions are not new. In 1856 the Hogg Brothers, John and William, advertised their Hogg's Hollow project while Angus Blue promoted another scheme, to be built on the east side of Yonge north of Sheppard, the following year.

• In the summer of 1914 a "flax festival" was held in the fields near the corner of Yonge and Ellerslie streets. Flax grown here was woven into linen that was used to cover the wings of biplanes built in Toronto.

• Irish immigrant Timothy Eaton opened his first Toronto store in 1869 at the southwest corner of Yonge and Queen streets where The Bay (formerly Simpson's) store now stands. Scottish-born Robert Simpson opened his first Toronto store on the northwest side of the same corner in 1872. The two businessmen switched places several years later. Eaton's is still on Yonge Street while Simpson's is no more, having been absorbed into the massive Hudson's Bay operation in 1978.

• Toronto's last duel was consummated near the corner of today's Yonge and College streets early in the morning of July 12, 1817. Poor John Ridout would never have to worry about a parking space or market value re-assessment again. He was shot to death by his opponent Samuel Jarvis.

• There was a plan put forward in 1953 to make the Toronto portion of Yonge Street a one-way thoroughfare, southbound to morning rush hour traffic, northbound in the evening.

• Johns have played an important part in the development of Yonge Street. No, not that kind of john. Rather, three early settlers, John Steele, John Finch, and John Willson (two "l"s please) are remembered in three major Yonge cross streets. Oh, and while we're doing a spell check, early maps show the Shepard family spelled their surname with only one "p".

• Over the years Yonge Street has had at least six cemeteries situated adjacent to it. Potter's Field at the Bloor Street intersection in 1826, St. Michael's just south of St. Clair avenue in 1855, the beautiful Mt. Pleasant in 1876, historic St. John's Anglican churchyard about 1817, York Cemetery in 1948, and the small Methodist Episcopal cemetery just south of the Nortown Plaza about 1834.

• In 1968 eleven North York councillors were in favour of changing the name of what was then known as the Borough of North York. Suggestions for a new name ranged from the Borough of Donnybrook to the Borough of Trudeau or Pluto. Some even suggested the title Borough of Yonge would be fitting. The latter idea was dropped when it was determined that many citizens would probably misspell Yonge.

Very early stages of Yonge subway construction north of Queen Street, 1949.

There's Plenty of Mileage on Tow-Truck Issue

February 25, 1996

I t always amazes me how often, while perusing the old *Toronto Telegram* newspaper looking for story ideas, I come across an item that, except for a picture used or prices quoted, could be an item from yesterday's *Sun*. Take the ongoing story about Metro's so-called tow truck "vultures" who charge, on the average, $250 to tow a vehicle from the scene of an accident. The Metro Licensing Commission is recommending a fee of $95 as more realistic for towing cars involved in accidents, with that fee to include the first ten kilometres of the tow. Disabled vehicles (other than those involved in accidents) would be towed for a Metro-wide flat fee of just $75.

Initially, one would think that this controversy is something new. However an advertisement for the Deluxe Towing Company in a February, 1927 edition of the newspaper reveals that the terror and torment of towing in Toronto is just another problem that only seems to be new. The De Luxe Towing Company was associated with the Deluxe Cab Company, one of the city's first taxi operators. Their ad says that Toronto motorists have long desired "a prompt, reliable towing service at reasonable charges" and that De Luxe now provides that service, day or night. One call to the company (phone MAin 6171) and a truck "with an expert mechanic in charge will be dispatched at once."

As far as towing fees were concerned, if the disabled vehicle was within the Toronto city limits its owner would pay $1 to get the tow truck there, plus an additional 50¢ a mile to get the car towed back to either of the De Luxe garages, centrally located at 251 Queen Street East and 1355 Queen Street West, or to any other repair shop requested by the driver. Interestingly, that mechanic who attended each and every call would, if requested, carry out repairs on the spot, charging 10¢ for every three minutes he (sorry, no female mechanics on staff back then) worked on the vehicle. A half-hour to fix the problem, another buck.

Now if your car happened to conk out while you were rambling through the countryside out near Duncan's Corners (now the Don Valley Parkway/York Mills Road interchange), Scarborough Junction (near Eglinton

Your disabled car towed at moderate rates!

MOTORISTS have wanted a prompt, reliable towing service at reasonable charges. De Luxe now provides this convenience and already have earned the patronage — and the gratitude — of hundreds of Toronto motorists.

Simply telephone our office and a special truck will leave at once, with an expert mechanic in charge. Within a short time your disabled car will be back in your own garage or in the repair shop you specify.

If you compare rates, you'll choose De Luxe.

De Luxe
Towing Service
251 Queen St. E.
1355 Queen St. W.

Deluxe Towing Service's 1927 newspaper advertisement.

and Kennedy), or at Highfield, which was not far from the Brown's Line/Old Malton Road intersection (these latter thoroughfares are now Highway 427 and Rexdale Boulevard) the charges were slightly different. The company charged a flat $1 plus a mileage charge of 50¢ a mile to and from the car whether a tow was required or not. However, the actual repair charge remained the same as a city break-down. Remember? A dime every three minutes.

While at first glance one might conclude that these figures are absurdly low remember that a good annual wage back then was about $1,000, a figure that wasn't much more than the price of one of Henry Ford's new Model "A"s.

* * * * *

Here's a rather unusual request. *Sunday Sun* reader Andrew Cobean writes to ask whether anyone remembers the name of the steer that led cattle from the holding pens at the southwest corner of St. Clair Avenue and Keele Street (now the site of a massive Home Depot store) across St. Clair to the slaughter house on the north side. The steer would then return to the pens to lead more cattle to their ultimate fate. Gotta name? Drop me a line.

Following the appearance of this article I received a number of suggestions as to just what this poor animal's name was. The vast majority thought it was "Judas" (though that was a goat, the "Judas goat") while one reader suggested "General." Any other ideas?

OH, TO BE IN ENGLAND...

March 3, 1996

Here I sit at my desk wondering what to write about for this week's column. Outside it's overcast and drizzling. Not winter and not really spring. Actually, it's nothing. My car's dirty and the bottom of my overcoat and all my shoes are encrusted with salt. Yech!

Wish I was doing what I was doing exactly six months ago. And what was that you ask? I was roaming the backroads of England eagerly searching out the numerous Toronto "connections" scattered throughout that glorious land.

I had developed this concept of a "Torontonian's tour of England" a year or so ago and through the facilities of Year Round Travel in North York I was able to stimulate a troop of a dozen other local history buffs enough to pay their fare and accompany me. Rather than hooking up with a existing tour, I concocted my own itinerary and called upon the services of the people at Backroads Touring in London to supply us with a small fourteen-passenger mini-bus and the friendliest, most accommodating driver/escort I have ever had the pleasure of meeting. In retrospect, there's no doubt that Nigel made the trip an absolute success.

Our first "port of call" was Wolford Chapel in Devon wherein lie the remains of Ontario's first lieutenant-governor and our city's founder, John Graves Simcoe. Nearby are those of his wife Elizabeth, who captured the early years of our community so vividly in her fascinating diary, and those of five of the eleven Simcoe children. The chapel and the land on which it rests are now part of Ontario, and the Ontario Heritage Foundation is responsible for the 194-year-old chapel's upkeep.

I had arranged for Chris Dracott, the expert on Simcoe's life in England before and after his tenure in Upper Canada, to accompany us on a tour around Devon. We visited several family churches (boy, has England got churches!!) and lunched in the pub frequented by Simcoe.

Later in the tour we'd visit the house in Cotterstock where Simcoe was born, as well as the nearby church he attended as a boy. On the church wall is a beautifully engraved marble plaque to his father, after whom the governor named our Lake Simcoe.

Another highlight of our ramble was a visit to Toronto, a tiny hamlet near

"Filey's Followers" at the Great House in Colyton. It was here that Sir George Yonge lived much of his life.

Bishop Auckland in Durham. It was originally known as Newton Cap until the owner of the nearby coal mine, who was attending a meeting in our city when word arrived that a new coal seam had been discovered, promptly changed the name of the community to honour Toronto. Here we dined at the Toronto Lodge operated by the world's most intense Blue Jay fan. Oh, how he must have suffered last year.

Arriving in Seaton, a small town on the south coast after which Sir John Colborne (Colborne Street, Colborne Lodge in High Park) took the title Lord Seaton (Seaton Street), we traveled on a diminutive tram (we call them streetcars) a few miles inland to the pretty little village of Colyton where Sir George Yonge (of two-hundred-year-old Yonge Street fame) is buried. The town's local history buff is attempting to track down Yonge family members for me. Stay tuned.

The absolute highlight of the tour was visiting the senior retirement homes in Exeter, Southampton, and Liverpool, each of which has the name Toronto in its title. This identification honours the thousands of readers of the *Toronto Evening Telegram* newspaper who raised money through bake sales, street carnivals, bridge tournaments, etc. The money, totalling almost $3 million (a huge amount in those bleak war years), was directed to the Lord Mayor of London's Air Raid Distress Fund where it was used to build new homes for those had lost theirs during the incessant German air raids. Eight other cities have similar "Toronto" facilities.

At each location we visited we were met by the local mayor, other civic dignitaries, and residents. TV and radio crews appeared and commemorative plaques were unveiled. In Liverpool a maple tree was planted to honour those who helped provide shelter for the blitz victims. The people of England still remember!

Oops, the sun's come out. Gotta go wash the car. I'll resume the story in a future column. By the way, if you think this is the kind of trip you'd like to go on, drop me a note. Perhaps we'll do another one. Maybe one to Scotland as well.

PS. Next Wednesday will be our city's 162nd birthday. Happy Birthday Toronto, in advance.

I hope to repeat this tour several times in the future. If it's something you'd like more information about, drop me a line c/o the publisher of this book.

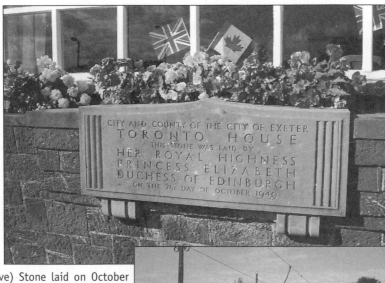

(Above) Stone laid on October 21, 1949 by the then Princess Elizabeth at Toronto House in Exeter. Note the Canadian flag in the window.

(Right) Diminutive tram connecting Seaton and Colyton

CLEARING THE WAY FOR YONGE STREET

March 10, 1996

Lost in all the hoopla surrounding the Yonge Street two-hundredth anniversary party is the fascinating story about surveyor Augustus Jones who was responsible for charting the pioneer thoroughfare's route through the dense forest that surrounded York (the tiny community that grew into today's Metropolitan Toronto) and the small band of Queen's Rangers who did the exhausting, back-breaking work of carving the street's initial "34 miles and 53 chains" through the wilderness.

According to the Dictionary of Canadian Biography, Augustus Jones was born in the Hudson River valley, New York in either 1757 or 1758 (official documents are imprecise on the actual year). As a young man he trained as a land surveyor in New York City, but with the end of the War of Independence, Augustus, accompanied by his father and several brothers and sisters, all of whom were determined to remain loyal to the King of England, moved to the new "loyalist settlements" located in the Niagara Peninsula.

In a drawing by C.W. Jefferys (1869–1951), an artist who lived in a house that still stands on the east side of Yonge Street just north of York Mills Road, members of the Queen's Rangers are shown cutting the original Yonge Street through the forest north of York.

A few years later Augustus was sworn in as a "crown surveyor" and soon found himself hard at work surveying properties and land grants scattered throughout what, in 1791, would become the new Province of Upper Canada (renamed Ontario in 1867).

The man selected by the British government to guide the new province through its formative years, John Graves Simcoe, was impressed

Cutting out Yonge Street 1795
—C.W. Jefferys Collection, Public Archives of Canada

Sir George Yonge 1731-1812

with the young surveyor's talents, and using his influence the lieutenant-governor saw to it that Jones was elevated to the important position of provincial Deputy Surveyor General when that position became vacant.

In his new position Jones was responsible for surveying town plots, lands along the Grand River, and townships from today's Fort Erie to Burlington and Hamilton. In fact, it was said that during the period 1787–1795 no other surveyor measured and subdivided so much important land in Upper Canada as did Augustus Jones.

Jones was also responsible for the laying out of two strategic military roads; the first from the Town of York to the Detroit frontier and the second from York to the Pine Fort on today's Holland River, a watercourse that connects, via Lake Simcoe and the Severn River, with Georgian Bay and the upper Great Lakes. The two trails were named in honour of prominent English statesmen of the time, Sir Henry Dundas and Sir George Yonge, respectively.

Working in the harshest winter weather (when the ground was firm and the leaves were off the trees, resulting in optimum sightlines) Jones became as proficient with snowshoes as he was with a fully laden canoe.

He retired from government service in 1800 and took up farming, still retaining his militia captaincy. Jones busied himself in selling off much of the land he had acquired over the years. He died near Paris, Ontario in 1837.

While Jones was responsible for the surveying of the route to be followed by Simcoe's military trail to the north, it was a thirty member contingent of the Queen's Rangers who actually cleared the way. The Rangers had been established by Simcoe in December of 1791 to assist with the task of colonizing and protecting the new province. The document authorizing the creation of the Queen's Rangers (the name perpetuated the corps Simcoe had commanded during the American Revolutionary War) had been signed three months earlier by none other that the Secretary of War himself, Sir George Yonge. In that letter Yonge defined, among other things, that a Ranger must be not less than 5' 4" in height and between 16 and 30 years of age. Sir George also specified that one of the new corps duties would be to "assist in the formation of Roads of Communication". To show his gratitude Simcoe named one of these "roads of communication" Yonge Street.

The Queen's Rangers are perpetuated today by the Queen's York Rangers (1st American Regiment), members of which have been active in Cyprus, Namibia and Bosnia.

WEARIN' O' THE GREEN

March 17, 1996

Happy St. Patrick's Day everyone! How's that old saying go? There are really only two nationalities, those who are Irish and those who wish they were. Interestingly, St. Patrick's name appears v ery early in the history of our city. In fact, it was exactly 162 years ago last Wednesday, March 6, 1834, that his name was first used to designate one of the newly created City of Toronto's five political wards. In addition to Patrick, patron saints (and their countries) Andrew (Scotland), David (Wales), George (England), and Lawrence — actually Laurence — (Canada), were similarly recognized in ward identification.

But even earlier than that, a little touch of Ireland was evident in this part of British North America when the land along the north shore of Lake Ontario between today's Bay of Quinte and the Humber River was divided into eleven "townships." One of the townships was designated Dublin. That township's name was later altered to York in recognition of the nearby Town of York that Simcoe had established on the north shore of Toronto Bay (it was always Toronto Bay) in 1793. It's from the town's name that the titles of the present cities of North York and York, as well as the Borough of East York, are derived. Had the township's original title not been changed to York sometime in the early 1800s it's conceivable that my wife and I would be living with Mayor Mel and nearly a half-a-million other souls in the City of North Dublin, a community flanked on the east and west, respectively, by the City of Dublin and the Borough of East Dublin.

Then there's St. Patrick's Roman Catholic Church on St. Patrick's Street in downtown Toronto. Actually, when the original church was erected in the early 1860s, the thoroughfare on which it was built was called William Street, after William Dummer Powell, a local landowner. The present structure dates from 1870.

And what about St. Patrick's Market? "St. Patrick's what?" you ask. In 1837 D'Arcy Boulton Jr. offered a piece of property on the north side of Queen Street just west of McCaul to the city fathers on the condition that a market be erected thereon to serve the citizens living in the western extremities of the small city (those living closer to the city centre at the King and Church corner having their own St. Lawrence Market to attend). Adhering to Boulton's terms, the city still operates a much-gentrified St. Patrick's Market on the Queen Street property.

And then there was the Toronto St. Pats professional hockey team. Originally known as the Arenas (because the team played at the Arena on Mutual Street), the name change was made in 1919 in hopes that huge numbers of Irish Torontonians would buy tickets. In 1927 the team name was changed again, this time to the Toronto Maple Leafs.

We've even had riots on St. Patrick's Day, one of the most serious occurring in 1878 following the appearance of O'Donovan Rossa, a fiery Fenian who greatly antagonized the Protestant Irish in Toronto. Crowds of Orangemen gathered outside the St. Lawrence Hall where Rossa was to speak, and when it was discovered that he had escaped their wrath dressed as a woman, every window in the building was smashed. Then it was on to the hotel of well-known Irish sympathizer Owen Cosgrove at the corner of, where else, Queen and St. Patrick streets where the mob proceeded to wreck the place. To give equal time to the Orange Order, their July 12 parades also had a tendency to erupt in donnybrooks. But that's another story for another time.

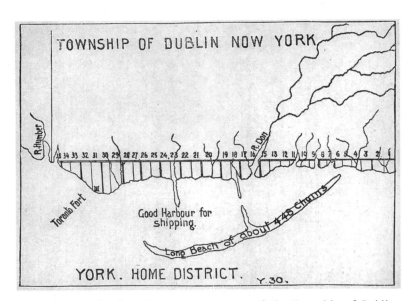

Map of 1796 showing the proposed survey of the Township of Dublin, renamed the Township of York. Lot numbers 1 through 35 are seen fronting on what was Lot Street (today's Queen Street).

From Downs View to Downsview

March 24, 1996

On March 30, 1954, forty-two years ago this coming Saturday, the first twelve stations on Toronto's brand new Yonge subway line opened to huge throngs of passengers eager to ride Canada's first subway.

Next Friday, March 29, the system's sixty-sixth station (some individual stations count as two, e.g. Yonge/Bloor) will open as the terminus of the Spadina line is extended two kilometres northward to a new station east of the Sheppard/Allen Road intersection. This station holds the dubious distinction of being the last subway station to be built in Metro this century.

Interestingly, when it came time to name the new Spadina subway station two seemingly obvious names quickly came to mind. *Sheppard West* was one, *Wilson Heights* another. However, when the community was asked for its input, the history of the area took precedence and the name Downsview was put forward. Acceding to the community's wish the TTC announced that the new station would, in fact, be called Downsview. Oh, by the way, not that I want to throw cold water on this consensus, but shouldn't it be Downs View? Why? read on.

Perkins Bull's Downs View farmhouse still stands, albeit much modernized, as the North Park Nursing Home at 450 Rustic Road in North York.

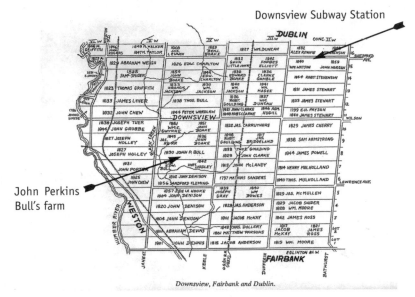

Downsview Subway Station

John Perkins
Bull's farm

Downsview, Fairbank and Dublin.

This map of the Downsview area appears in *Pioneering in North York* by Patricia Hart (published for the North York Historical Society in 1968 by General Publishing). It shows the location of John Perkins Bull's Downs View Farm and the site of the TTC's new Downsview subway station.

In 1818 Bartholemew Bull and his family left Ireland seeking a better future in the "new world." Bartholemew Bull eventually purchased two hundred acres of land in the rural hinterland of York Township, identified on maps of the day as simply Lot 8, Concession IV West. Today, this property would be described as all the land surrounded by Keele Street, Maple Leaf Drive, Jane Street and Falstaff Avenue.

When Bartholemew's son, John Perkins Bull, graduated from Victoria College, the proud father gave the young man the two-hundred-acre property on which the twenty-year-old erected a small log cabin in 1842. John proudly named his "estate" Downs View Farm. The first word in the title, "downs," is defined in the dictionary as being "open, rolling upland with fairly smooth slopes usually covered with grass" and was obviously selected to describe the view the Bull family had of the surrounding countryside.

The cabin John had built was replaced in about 1843 with a substantial brick dwelling that still stands, in much altered form, as the North Park Nursing Home at 450 Rustic Drive. In 1844, John married Caroline Carpenter.

Over the years the family farm house served not only as a residence, but as a court house and jail (John Perkins Bull held the position of justice of the peace for thirty-five years) and as the neighbourhood Wesleyan Methodist church. However, as the congregation grew the farm house parlour became too small, and a log structure was erected on the nearby dusty concession road, a road we now call Keele Street. In 1870 the log church was demolished and replaced on the same site by the pretty little Downsview United Church that still stands at 2822 Keele Street.

It wasn't long before the community surrounding the Bull property adopted the farm's name — although the double-barrel Downs View became simply Downsview.

Another use of the term Downsview describes the sprawling airport on the north side of Wilson Avenue. It began as a composite of several pioneer Toronto airfields, the first being the 220-acre flying field of Canadian Air Express that opened on the east side of Dufferin Street north of Wilson in 1928. A year later the de Havilland Aircraft factory moved from its Trethewey Avenue site, opening a seventy-acre airfield on the south side of Sheppard between Dufferin and Keele streets. The company referred to it as Downsview Airport. In 1931, the Toronto Flying Club moved from its Leaside location and opened a 220-acre field on the north side of Wilson east of Dufferin Street.

In 1947 the federal government expropriated large parcels of land in the area for "flightways" and road diversions, and RCAF Station Downsview came into being. Five years later the de Havilland field was purchased for $5 million and the company subsequently erected the present factory at the southwest limits of the sprawling airport. Most of "CFB Toronto" and much of the airport property are now being given back to the community.

PUTTING THE CITY'S PAST INTO FOCUS

March 31, 1996

One of the "extras" I get out of writing this column (which, incidentally I've done for more than twenty years now) is getting a phone call or letter right out of the blue offering me either old photographs or books depicting Toronto as it used to be. Here's a case in point. Recently a reader, who was cleaning out some cupboards, came across some old photographs. Before she just threw them into the garbage, she was kind enough to call me. When I went to take a look at what she had found I came across a couple of trays of colour slides taken around town in the late 50s/early 60s. Now, while that may not seem so very long ago, nevertheless it's amazing to see some of the "landmarks" we've lost just in that short span of time. Thanks to that reader's kindness, I'd like to share a trio of those views with you. And while the originals are in colour, they're reproduced here in good old-fashion black and white. The dates are "guestimates," two of which are based on the cars in the view.

1) The University Avenue Armouries, photo c.1959. Located where the Court House now stands on the east side of the street just north of Queen, this medieval-looking structure was erected in 1891–93 to house the city's various militia groups. It was here that citizen-soldiers signed-up to serve their country during the turn-of-the-century Boer War and the two world wars.

University Avenue
Armouries

Gooderham and Worts windmill replica

The modernization of the city, and the street, combined with the need for more courtroom space close to Osgoode Hall, sealed the Armoury's fate and it was demolished in 1963. Armoury Street recalls the structure.

2) Gooderham and Worts windmill replica, photo c.1958. When the Worts and Gooderham families first went into business in 1832, world-famous alcoholic beverages were still many years in the future. Actually, the company's first product was flour produced from grain, which was shipped to the site from the farms that surrounded the Town of York. The grinding was done by millstones propelled into action by the winds that rushed across Toronto Bay and were caught by the huge vanes of the company windmill (located south of today's Mill and Trinity street intersection). More reliable steam power replaced the windmill in about 1835, but the structure, re-roofed and without vanes, stood for several more years before being demolished. In 1954 a scaled down replica of the old landmark was erected at the southeast corner of Parliament Street and Lake Shore Boulevard, but with the coming of the Gardiner Expressway in the early 60s it too was flattened.

3) *S.S. Cayuga*, photo c.1955. After a visit to Toronto's waterfront it's difficult to believe that not too many decades ago the harbour was frequently chock full of freighters, tankers, and passenger ships. Of this latter category, there's no question that the most popular was *Cayuga*. Built for the forerunner of Canada Steamship Lines (CSL) and launched in 1906 at Bertram's Bathurst Street ship yard (not far from today's Front Street corner), *Cayuga* was not just the most popular passenger ship; it was also the one that lasted the longest, plying the Toronto–Niagara-on-the-Lake/Queenston/Lewiston route until retired from

S.S. Cayuga

service in 1957. This photo shows the vessel in Cayuga Steamship Company colours. This organization, with Alan Howard as its general manager, took over when CSL decided to get rid of the vessel. Unfortunately, even Alan's group couldn't alter declining revenues and mounting costs. *Cayuga* was scrapped in 1961.

* * * * *

The Weston Historical Society has recently published two books chock full of reminiscences of the early days in and around Weston (Volume 2 deals with Christmases past in old Weston). The books are available for $7.50 each (including tax and postage) from P.O. Box 79696, Old Weston Post Office, 1995 Weston Rd. M9N 3W9. And while we're visiting Weston, that community's historic Central United Church on King Street is celebrating its 175th anniversary this year. There'll be a Homecoming dinner and dance on May 4 and a special anniversary church service the following day. Interested? Call Eric Lee at (416) 741-3025 for additional details.

ARCHITECT LEAVES HIS LANDMARKS

April 7, 1996

What do all the following structures have in common: Jarvis Street Baptist Church (at the northeast corner of Gerrard Street), the former Robert Simpson store (now The Bay at the southwest corner of Yonge and Queen streets), the Prince Edward viaduct (to give the massive structure connecting Bloor Street with the Danforth its official title), and the CITY-TV/Much Music building on Queen Street West?

Give up?

All bear the signature of one of Toronto's most prolific and talented architects: Edmund Burke, who, like so many of our citizens who are successful in their chosen fields, remained virtually unknown here at home. But now Edmund Burke's life and times are the subject of a newly published book, *Toronto Architect: Edmund Burke* (McGill-Queen's University Press, $44.95). The author of this insightful and generously illustrated work, Carleton University assistant art professor Angela Carr, gives the reader a fascinating look into a period of Canadian history when buildings of architectural excellence could only be created by an Englishman — or at the very least, by an American. Back then native-born Canadian architects didn't really count. Toronto-born Edmund Burke helped change all that.

Edmund Burke's "memorial," the Prince Edward Viaduct.

Born in Toronto in 1850, Burke was the son of a general contractor and dealer in builders' supplies, and the nephew of Henry Langley, an established Toronto architect, Burke spent just two years at Upper Canada College before obtaining a junior apprentice position with his uncle Henry's firm at the ripe old age of 14.

The years went by, and as Edmund became more and more experienced he was offered a full partnership with his uncle, Henry Langley. Langley's firm expanded even further when, in 1873, another uncle, Toronto contractor Edward Langley, joined the duo, creating the respected firm of Langley, Langley & Burke, Canadian architects and builders.

In 1874, Burke's first independently produced architectural work was selected for the new Jarvis Street Baptist Church which opened

Toronto architect Edmund Burke (1850–1919)

the following year in the residential section of the city in and around the Jarvis and Gerrard street intersection.

Impressed with Burke's creation the church's benefactor, William McMaster, called on the architect a few years later to design the Toronto Baptist College for a site on the south side of Bloor Street, just west of the present Royal Ontario Museum. In 1887 the building was renamed McMaster College. It now houses the Royal Conservatory of Music.

In 1895 Burke introduced the modern "curtain-wall" concept to Canada, incorporating it in his design for Robert Simpson's new and "totally fireproof" downtown Toronto department store. The structure is now The Bay's Yonge and Queen store. It was, at the time, the most modern commercial design anywhere in the world.

One of the most interesting of Burke's many commissions was his contribution to the viaduct that soars over the Rosedale ravine and Don Valley connecting Bloor Street with Danforth Avenue. This mile-long lifeline connecting communities on the east and west banks of the valley was first proposed in the 1880s, but construction costs were far too great for the young city.

Financial concerns were not the only barrier to the project, however. Even back then environmental concerns and the beauty of the ravine and valley settings were important. Sensitive to these concerns the prestigious Toronto Civic Art Guild submitted a concept in 1909 but it too was rejected (as were proposals put forward in 1910 and 1912, the latter consisting of ideas received from around the world). In 1913, when the design submitted by the city's own Department of Public Works, received the go ahead city officials had the good sense to hire Edmund Burke to act as architectural consultant thereby ensuring that the massive new concrete and steel viaduct complimented the setting rather than detracting from it.

Burke demonstrated his concerns for other big city problems and frequently offered his ideas for new road layouts and various urban redevelopment schemes including the age-old plan to improve the Exhibition grounds.

Edmund Burke died on January 2, 1919, just a few months before the viaduct (which was officially renamed the Prince Edward Viaduct to commemorate the popular prince's visit to Toronto later that same year) opened to traffic. Burke was buried in Mt. Pleasant Cemetery.

GOING ON LOCATION AT EATON HALL

April 14, 1996

A new motion picture, *Mrs. Winterbourne* starring Shirley MacLaine, debuts at Toronto theatres next Friday. Also "starring" in the movie is one of southern Ontario's most magnificent landmarks. Located off north Dufferin Street not far from King City, *Eaton Hall* has a particularly interesting connection with Toronto, as it was to this country residence that the widow of Sir John Craig Eaton — son of the company founder and president of the T. Eaton Company from 1907 until 1922 — moved after her husband's tragic demise at the young age of 45.

Interestingly, it was while the young couple was living in their now-demolished *Ardwold* estate, which stood just north of Sir Henry Pellatt's Casa Loma (today's Ardwold Gate retains the estate's Irish title), that they first heard about the magnificent King Township property from their neighbour, who was soon to abandon his castle and move to new digs out in the tranquility and privacy of the township.

The Eatons talked about building a new country residence on the farm just east of Sir Henry's, but plans were cut short when Sir John died suddenly, years later. Lady Eaton eventually went ahead with the construction of her new home moving into the magnificent *Eaton Hall* in 1938. Eventually old

Eaton Hall

Lady Eaton "at the hunt" on her Eaton Hall property, 1945.

age and ill health forced Lady Eaton to move back to the conveniences of the city and *Eaton Hall* was closed. Following her death in 1971 Seneca College purchased the 696-acre estate and converted the former residence into classrooms and offices. When the campus expanded in 1978 the building became the college's Management Development Centre. In 1993 it took on another new role as Seneca College's Eaton Hall Inn and Conference Centre.

* * * * *

Several weeks ago an especially significant event in the long and fascinating saga of public transit in our city occurred when the last of the TTC's once omnipresent Presidents' Conference Committee (PCC) streetcars glided into the carhouse on December 8, 1995 to conclude the nearly sixty years of faithful service provided by this unique type of transit vehicle. (To the Commission's credit, a pair of PCCs have been retained for special ceremonial and charter service.)

While three Canadian cities, Montreal, Vancouver, and Toronto operated almost eight hundred new and used PCCs, fleets in cities south of the border had almost three thousand of them. There were hundreds more in European cities and countless (literally) numbers throughout countries of the former Soviet Union. In South America, Tocopilla, Chile and Buenos Aires, Argentina operated "second hand" PCC cars, and even Melbourne, Australia (where, like Toronto, streetcars are still important transit vehicles) had a pair of PCC cars in service.

When the TTC reluctantly decided late last year to abandon PCC operations, eighteen PCC cars (fourteen rebuilt and four unrefurbished) were offered for sale. The Commission wisely kept a pair for special charter and ceremonial uses.

After assessing the bids three rebuilt PCCs, plus two unrefurbished cars, were sold to a consortium of seven American trolley museums. A museum in Wisconsin purchased the remaining rebuilt PCC car. One unrefurbished PCC was sold to a local broker (this car's ultimate fate is unknown at this time), while another unrefurbished vehicle will be shipped to a scrap dealer in Hamilton. Three lots of PCC parts were purchased by the San Francisco, California city public transit operator so that eventually a little bit of Toronto will be plying the streetcar routes of the Golden Gate city.

The PCC era in Toronto is available on a two-hour videotape from GPS Video, Box 5895, Postal Station "A", Toronto M5W 1P3. Also from GPS Video are sixty-minute video tributes to "Roncesvalles Carhouse 100th Anniversary" and to the "Lansdowne Carhouse, 1911–1996".

SWIMMER FINALLY GETS HIS DUE

April 21, 1996

On May 4, 1996 marathon swimmer George Young will be inducted, posthumously, into the Ontario Aquatic Hall of Fame in the "Pioneer Swimmer" category. Swim Ontario, the governing body that administers the Hall of Fame, is eager to have George's relatives present at the ceremony. Unfortunately, time has obscured any trace of them. Should you know of any family members please call Swim Ontario at (416) 426-7224.

George Young was born in Aberdeen, Scotland in 1910 and was just three when he and his recently widowed mother emigrated to Canada. They took up residence in an upstairs flat at 248 Lippincott Street, and though they were poor, they were happy. Without a lot of spare money around George soon found that the one thing his mother could afford was a membership at the West End YMCA at College and Dovercourt. George loved to swim and by the time he was 10 had come under the expert tutelage of one of the country's best-known swimming coaches: Johnny Walker.

As the years went by George's powerfully developed shoulder muscles made the choice of long distance swimming obvious. By the time he had turned 18 he had won Montreal's "St. Lawrence River bridge-to-bridge" marathon three times, Toronto "across the bay" competition four times (the first time when he was just 13), and the particularly grueling Eastern Channel to Western Channel contest twice.

Late in 1926 George read somewhere that the Wrigley gum people were offering the incredible sum of $25,000 to the first person to swim the twenty-two miles of frigid water between Catalina Island and the California mainland. Imagine! Getting that much money for doing something that he could do better than just about anyone else was all the incentive seventeen-year-old George needed.

But getting money for the trip was nearly impossible. Even his coach's plea for assistance fell on deaf ears. Nevertheless, George and Bill Hastings, his swimming buddy from the "Y," were able to borrow a few dollars from Mrs. Young. After fixing up their beaten-up Henderson motorcycle the boys were soon on their way. Strapped for cash, George even had the nerve to stop at

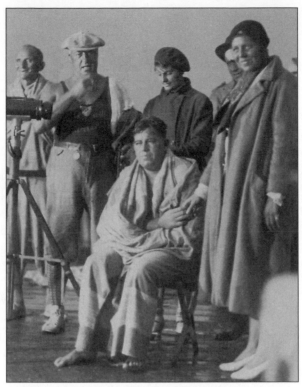

George Young, winner of the 1931 CNE Marathon Swim with his coach, Johnny Walker, and mother. This success was greeted with little enthusiasm by Torontonians who remembered his failure four years before.

the Wrigley office in Chicago and borrow $60 from William Wrigley, Jr., the man who was sponsoring the race.

George finally reached Catalina and at 11:23 in the morning of January 15, 1927 began slicing through the frigid water headed for the California mainland more than twenty miles away.

Nearly sixteen hours later George crawled ashore. He had done it! Not only had the unknown seventeen-year-old Torontonian won the Catalina Channel Derby and the $25,000, but he was the only person of the 102 participants (some the world's best) to finish the grueling assignment.

Upon his return to Toronto, George was given a reception the likes of which were usually only accorded royalty. To most people, George was nothing less than superhuman. And when it was announced that Wrigley would bring his swim to the CNE that summer it was naturally assumed that George would win that one too. But he didn't, and in the eyes of his fickle public George quickly went from hero to a "gutless bum." George finally won the CNE marathon in 1931 (almost drowning in the process), but the feelings of adulation and respect accorded the young man years earlier were never rekindled. And it turned out that poor George had been cheated out of most of his winnings, sued by various and sundry people and on the outs with various members of the family. George Young, who, for a fleeting moment was a Toronto "superstar," died virtually unknown in Niagara Falls, Ontario in 1972. On May 4, George will finally get the recognition he deserves.

As a result of this article George's step son contacted Swim Ontario and was subsequently present at the induction ceremony to accept the tribute to his father.

BRINGING THE WORLD INTO FOCUS

April 28, 1996

L ast week Kodak Canada introduced something brand new in the ever changing field of photography. Advantix, Kodak's name for the revolutionary "advanced photo system," has a number of features that will be welcomed by the most amateur of amateur photographers. There's no fumbling with threading the film leader (there is none), getting the exposed film out of the camera, setting the film speed, using the flash, etc. etc. Everything's automatic. Prints from the new, slightly smaller than 35mm film are improved, films are more versatile, and now three different picture formats (standard, wide angle and panoramic) on the same roll of film, in any order, are possible.

And the system has a really neat feature for those of us who take a lot of pictures and then promptly scratch and/or misplace the negatives. With the new system the delicate negatives are never touched. After processing you receive, in addition to your prints, negatives in a closed canister and an index print that has thumbnail-size images of all the pictures on that roll. You reorder by selecting a number from your thumbnail images, and never have to peer at or even touch the negatives. The canisters and index cards can be stored in a special album. So as advanced as the new system may be it would appear that the old company slogan "you press the button, we do the rest" is as true today as it was in 1899 when George Eastman decided to expand his Kodak operation into Canada.

In fact less than two decades had passed since the twenty-six-year-old Rochester, New York bank clerk had become a pioneer in the fledgling photographic world when he perfected a process for making dry photographic plates, a definite improvement on the then-standard wet plates. In 1884, Eastman triumphed again when he invented a machine that turned out photographic paper in long rolls which, four years later, made possible his new "roll film" camera, a product that was far more convenient to use than the those of the cumbersome and expensive "dry plate" variety. In fact, now anyone could take pictures, even Canadians. And so in 1899 Eastman decided to take his products north of the border.

Kodak Canada was chartered as Canadian Kodak Company Ltd. on

The former Kodak factory complex at 582–592 King Street West soon after the company's move to Mt. Dennis. These old Kodak buildings still stand (inset).

November 3, 1899 and within a few weeks the first plant was up and running in downtown Toronto at 41 Colborne Street. Here bulk film and photographic paper received from the Rochester operation was cut, spooled, packaged, and shipped to the few photographic supply dealers then in business.

Photography, for both professionals and amateurs, grew dramatically and soon the original premises became overcrowded, resulting in a new building being erected at 588 King Street West near Portland (see photos) in 1901. Although two additional buildings were constructed nearby it wasn't long before this downtown location became unsuitable as well. Realizing the problem, in 1913 George Eastman, the company founder, came to Toronto to supervise the choice of a new site.

This time a twenty-five-acre parcel of land well out in the countryside was selected. The site was ideal, partially because the property was served by a railway line, and also because it was close to Eglinton Avenue and Weston Road — two thoroughfares that, in those far-off days, were just dusty country roads intersecting at a place called Mount Dennis. Here expansion could take place with ease.

In 1914 construction of the first seven buildings at what became known locally as Kodak Heights began, and by the spring of 1917 all operations had been transferred to the sprawling new location from the cramped downtown site.

Over the years Kodak Canada Inc. (the name was streamlined in 1979) has been involved in the manufacture of a variety of photographic products. Today, the Kodak Heights facility has the corporation's world mandate to manufacture micrographic film. In addition, a myriad of other Kodak products are shipped nationwide from the Mt. Dennis site.

Kodak founder George Eastman (1854–1932).

THAT'S MAYTIME ENTERTAINMENT

May 5, 1996

P re-television Torontonians looking for something to do on the evenings of either May 9 and 10, 1947 could choose from an array of movies playing at the many theatres in and around the city of the day. Interestingly, many of those films have become timeless screen classics. For instance, at Shea's on Bay Street (a site now partially occupied by Nathan Phillips Square and new City Hall) *It's a Wonderful Life* was held over for a "second fabulous week," while at the Tivoli at the corner of Richmond and Victoria *The Jolson Story* was in its eighth week. Uptown at the Uptown *The Egg and I* was still going strong after five weeks. On the other side of Yonge Street the Embassy (now the New Yorker, home of the fabulous *Four Plaids*) was screening the immensely forgettable *Black Parachute* and *One More Tomorrow* on its double bill. And while on the subject of forgettable out in the suburbs the Scarborough Theatre on Kingston Road had *Two Guys from Milwaukee* (who looked suspiciously like Dennis Morgan and Jack Carson), while in Etobicoke the timeless Kingsway Theatre featured *Make Mine Music* and *Abilene Town*. If an evening of dancing was more your speed how 'bout stopping by the Masonic Temple where Paul Firman's band was featured in the auditorium. Eddie Stroud and his orchestra were at the Savarin on Bay,

Sunnyside Stadium, home of Sunnyside Ladies Softball League and located on the south side of Lake Shore Boulevard (just to the east of what was the Parkdale Canoe Club and is now the Boulevard Club) was a baseball fan's delight from 1924 until the playing field and stands were replaced by a parking lot in the mid-1950s.

Jimmy Amaro at the St. Regis Hotel on Sherbourne, and Frank Perry and his Rambling Cowboys were over at the Orange Hall at the College and Euclid corner. Out of town Rudy Spratt was featured at Club 31 near Stop 31 on Kingston Road, up north George Smith was at the Cedar Beach pavilion on Musselman's Lake, and over Hamilton way Paul Page and his orchestra were at the Brant Inn.

As many choices as there were, many North Torontonians had already made plans for those evenings. Jack Dow, a newcomer to the teaching staff of North Toronto Collegiate Institute, had put together an evening of entertainment that would feature members of the school's orchestra and choir. Dubbed Maytime Melodies by the school's perennial English teacher Betty Bealey, the event would be held in the cramped confines of the school's ancient auditorium. The first selection rendered by the orchestra was the "Triumphal March from Aida," and the event concluded with an Irving Berlin medley arranged by the same Jack Dow. Over the next half-century Maytime Melodies evolved into the city's most popular high school concert. Next Sunday (May 12) a special fiftieth anniversary Maytime Melodies concert will be held at Roy Thomson Hall. For info on this event and on the pre-concert mini-reunion/silent auction, call the fiftieth anniversary hot-line: (416) 968-2734.

* * * * *

A new book from University of Toronto Press has just made it into the bookstores. *All I Thought About Was Baseball: Writings on a Canadian Pastime* ($24.95, softcover) is a collection of more than fifty stories — some fiction, some fact — prepared by some of the country's best-known writers: Morley Callahan, Hugh Hood, W.P. Kinsella, Marshall McLuhan, and Alison Gordon, with contributions from a number of other talented freelance writers. Interestingly, what most people accept as just another game imported from south of the border has a fascinating history right here in our country. In fact, a version of baseball was being played in Guelph, Ontario at almost the same instance that it was being "invented" in the States. One of the most interesting stories is by Laura Robinson. In it, she tells the story of the immensely popular ladies' softball league that, during the summers from 1924–1956, played hundreds of games at the old Sunnyside stadium that was located on the south side of Lake Shore Boulevard right where the Boulevard Club parking lot is today. Here the likes of "Buster" Nicholson, Irene Aldred and Flo Cutting playing for teams such as the Supremes, Cycles, Grottos, and Parksides gave their fans baseball every bit as good as the stuff seen at SkyDome — often better.

IMPROVING THE RAIL LANDS ON TRACK

May 12, 1996

I forget who uttered those immortal words, "stuff don't have to be old to be historic." Perhaps it was the same person who penned an equally interesting corollary to that statement, "what goes around, comes around."

A perfect example of an event in our community's relatively recent past that proves the validity of both statements was the massive redevelopment proposal for Toronto's railway lands that came to light on September 12, 1967. Had plans for the Metropolitan (later shortened to Metro) Centre project been implemented, the 185 acres between Yonge and Bathurst streets, south of Front Street, would have been covered with a multitude of new buildings, including a new postal centre, an 1,800-room hotel, and, replacing the stately Union Station, a modern transportation centre. Underground, miles of pedestrian malls would allow ant-like movement between buildings regardless of the weather outside.

Developers also hoped that the CBC would build its long proposed communication centre on the site, and as an incentive to get the CBC on side it was decided that the new project would include a 1,500-foot-high, two-legged broadcasting tower complete with an observation deck at the 1,200-foot level. While nameless at the time, nearly a decade later that same broadcasting facility (in a redesigned form and 315' 5" taller) became the city's newest landmark.

When introduced in late 1967, the Metropolitan Centre proposal was so mind-boggling in scale that the media found it necessary to equate the area it would cover as being the same as that covered by an eighteen-hole golf course. As it would turn out, an extremely interesting comparison.

As the project stumbled through the seemingly endless discussion process, political and public pressures combined to slowly strangle the project. One of the greatest roadblocks to the implementation of the original scheme became the public's demand that Union Station be retained *in its entirety*, a notion that the developers flatly rejected.

Thirty years have gone by and the original Metro Centre proposal is now part of our history, albeit our recent history. And in the interim, both

SkyDome and the expansion of the Metro Toronto Convention Centre have helped to improve both the appearance and use of the once-derelict railway lands. And as if to prove that what goes around comes around, it even looks like we'll get that golf course.

Mayor William Dennison beams as he shows off the model of Toronto's new Metropolitan Centre. Note the original CN Tower design. The then existing Royal York Hotel and Toronto-Dominion Centre towers are also visible. Metro Centre went the way of the dodo while the original tower design was changed drastically.

The addition to the Metro Toronto Convention Centre, which effectively doubled the size of the ultra-modern facility to two million square feet, was officially opened on July 16, 1997. The new section was constructed south of the original structure and is totally underground. The yet-to-be-restored 1928 CPR roundhouse, a new park, and several street extensions sit astride its massive roof.

Happy Twenty-Fifth, Ontario Place

May 19, 1996

I don't care how many times you tell me, it just doesn't seem possible. A whole quarter-of-a-century can't have gone by since Ontario Place opened to the public.

Well, as much as I want to disbelieve that last statement, the fact remains our city's waterfront jewel, Ontario Place, is exactly twenty-five years old this year having opened its gates for the first time May 22, 1971.

And while Ontario Place's actual birth may have taken place twenty-five years ago, the date of its conception is much older still. In fact, Ontario Place can be said to have had its origin during the six month run of the Canadian

In this view, taken on March 3, 1970 of what was initially referred to as Ontario Showplace, landfill for the islands, steelwork for the pods, and a breakwall consisting of stripped and sunken Great Lake freighter hulls are plainly visible. Across Lake Shore Boulevard on the grounds of the Canadian National Exhibition we can see (left to right) the Horticultural Building, Bandshell, Better Living Centre, Queen Elizabeth Building, Grandstand, Food Building, Coliseum complex, roller coaster, and Shell Tower (the latter pair now demolished).

Universal and International Exhibition (it's better remembered as Expo '67) that was held in Montreal from April 28 to October 27 in Canada's centennial year.

One of the most popular attractions at Expo '67 was the Ontario Pavilion, which came complete with an entranceway lined with huge granite blocks and a seventeen-minute multi-screen film (orchestrated by musicians from the famed Toronto Symphony Orchestra and edited by the same crew that worked on the 1962 Hollywood feature film *Mutiny on the Bounty*).

By the time the fair was over the Ontario Pavilion had been so well received that some suggested that the $8.5-million structure, complete with sixty-six foot by thirty foot high movie screen, should be carefully disassembled, shipped to Toronto, and rebuilt somewhere on Toronto Island. And as exciting as that idea may have seemed at first, it turned out to be totally impractical. Nevertheless, James Ramsay, one of several Ontario Pavilion commissioners (and father of the snappy $100,000 advertising campaign that asked "Ontario, is there any place you'd rather be?"), put forward a concept that would see the creation of something akin to the Expo pavilion somewhere in the Province of Ontario. The idea quickly caught the fancy of politicians and bureaucrats alike.

As a result, it really didn't come as much of a surprise when, as he officially opened the Canadian National Exhibition on August 16, 1968, Premier John Robarts announced that the province would immediately proceed with the creation of an entirely new Government of Ontario complex on newly created land along the CNE waterfront south of Lake Shore Boulevard. Robarts also suggested that the new facility would have a major role to play in accommodating the 1976 Olympic Games when, and if, they were awarded to Toronto.

While the Olympics wouldn't come to Toronto (surprise, surprise they too went to Montreal), the unique waterfront entertainment complex as foreseen by the premier would. In fact, it was just at a media conference held on March 10, 1969 — a mere seven months after Robarts' original announcement at the CNE opening day ceremonies — that the first details concerning the physical dimensions and appearance of the complex were revealed. On hand for the unveiling of the plans for the "Ontario Showplace" (as it was identified at the time) were Premier Robarts and the provincial Trade and Development Minister, Stanley Randall.

To be designed by the Toronto architectural firm of Craig, Zeidler and Strong the complex — covering a total of eighty acres, twenty-three of which would be "man-made" using fill from various downtown Toronto construction sites — would feature five two-storey pavilions housing Expo-style exhibits dealing with Ontario's past, present, and future. These glass and steel pavilions would rise from a series of man-made bays, and on the roofs of some provision would be made for outdoor dining facilities.

Other features planned for the new Ontario Showplace, which would eventually grow in size to ninety acres, forty-six of them "man-made," included a two-hundred-boat marina and a children's village and creative play area. And piggy-backing on the enormous popularity of the theatre at Expo '67, there would also be a ninety-foot-high domed theatre complete with an enormous screen for multi-image screenings. The theatre would be called Cinesphere. Interestingly, at this stage of the provincial attraction's development there was no mention made about featuring a startling new Canadian invention, something called IMAX, at Cinesphere.

During the media conference Premier Robarts identified the new waterfront attraction as "the forerunner of the city of tomorrow." He suggested that the bill for the Ontario Showplace complex would be an estimated $13 million, with the official opening to take place on May 24, 1971.

At least the date of the opening came in under the proposed figure.

PLAY IT AGAIN, FRANK

May 26, 1996

The other night, while having dinner at Diana Sweets with friends Joan and Phil Lewis, I mentioned that earlier in the day I had met with perennial Toronto dance band leader Frank Bogart. No sooner were the words out of my mouth when the lady at the next table piped up "did you say, Frank Bogart? Why he played at my daughter's wedding. And that was twenty some years ago! How is the dear man?" Well, for that lady's benefit, and for the benefit of the many hundreds of music lovers who remember Frank, this patriarch of the local music scene is in remarkably good health. Celebrating his eighty-first birthday today, Frank remains a keen enthusiast of the art of karate (he's a professor of martial arts and has a fourth-degree black belt). In fact, one whole room of his spacious Bathurst Street apartment is chock full of exercise equipment. I'd suggest that when you make a musical request of Frank Bogart, you'd better say please.

Frank was born in Woodstock, Ontario on May 26, 1915. As a youngster he spent some time in Galt, Ontario before moving with the family to Hamilton. While attending Central High School in the "Ambitious City," Frank joined schoolmate Fred Sweeney's dance band as the group's pianist. It was about this time that the musical styling of American pianist Eddie Duchin was beginning to revolutionize the dance band scene. Frank heard Duchin at Toronto's Palais Royale in 1933, and it was then and there that the young man decided that was the style for him as well.

Following his graduation from high school, Frank was on the move again, this time to Toronto where he joined the popular Ferde Mowry band. At the time Mowry, a native of Peterborough, Ontario, had one of the most successful bands in the country. When Frank joined the band in 1934 Mowry was in his third year on the bandstand at the popular Club Embassy on Bloor Street West at Belair. In addition to Mowry's sweet sound, something else that made the Embassy such a popular place was its truly unique dance floor, which was mounted on springs. Only recently was the building that housed the Club Embassy pulled down.

In the summer of 1940, after six years with the Mowry organization, Frank decided to strike out on his own, taking his newly formed band into the beautifully situated Brant Inn on the Burlington, Ontario waterfront. Before long, however, Frank was back in Toronto. In fact, the summer of 1940 was just fading into memory when on Saturday, October 5 Frank Bogart, his piano, and orchestra opened at the prestigious Granite Club on St. Clair Avenue. Little did Frank realize that he was embarking on a "gig" that would span more than half-a-century at both the club's mid-town site and, after 1972, at its new Bayview Avenue location. Frank's only absences from the club came in the years 1941–43, during which he and his orchestra performed at the Club Top Hat on Lake Shore Boulevard West, and the years 1949–50, during which the orchestra played in the Royal York Hotel's Imperial Room.

A few years ago Frank actually tried retirement and didn't like it. Some might say he's now busier than ever with his music and a second career in the brokerage business. Happy Birthday, Frank!

Club Top Hat on Lake Shore Boulevard at the northeast corner of Parkside Drive. It was here that Frank played from 1941–43. The popular Sunnyside dance hall, which was originally known as the Club Esquire, was demolished in the mid-1950s to make way for the Gardiner Expressway. The wording on the marquee announcing Cy McLean's popular dance band would be totally unacceptable today.

The ever young, ever popular Frank Bogart.

WHAT A GAS TO LOOK BACK AT PRICES

June 16, 1996

Here's a twist to the recent spate of stories on the subject of high gasoline prices and the resulting cries for inquiries into the possibility of price fixing by the big gas companies.

On January 11, 1934 Imperial Oil Limited ran a full-page ad in the Toronto papers, advising that the company would henceforth sell its Imperial Blue brand of automotive gasoline at "less than cost." Some cynics suggested that this marketing strategy had something to do with the fact that McMaster University's Professor K.W. Taylor was conducting an investigation under the Combines Investigation Act into the price of gasoline. Of course, company officials denied this accusation, countering that their action was a direct result of owners of independent gasoline stations purchasing product south of the border where a gallon of gas was significantly cheaper. This fact, coupled with the recent lowering of the exchange rate and abolition of the government's "dumping" duty, allowed the independent dealer to retail gasoline at a significantly lower price than the major brand companies. There was also some suggestion that Russian gasoline had entered the market stream, a possibility that was never proven.

To paraphrase one Imperial Oil official, the company decided to protect its business interests and their employees' futures by lowering the price of a gallon of their Imperial Blue brand of gasoline to 16.5¢, a figure that was below cost. Other major companies followed suit, and before long there was a full-blown gasoline price war. Remember those things? Needless to say, the big guys won the day and things eventually returned to normal with a gallon retailing at 21.5¢.

Incidentally, if you think that *gasoline* was awfully cheap back in 1934, remember that a brand new eight-cylinder Ford automobile went for less than $900, with that hated GST/PST combo still decades in the future. If you'd like to learn more about the history of gas stations you're invited to join the Canadian Service Station Memorabilia Association. You can contact the CSSMA by writing Peter Ledwith, RR#4, Rockwood, ON. N0B 2K0.

* * * * *

The Good Rich gas station at the southeast corner of Dundas Street and Spadina Avenue, c.1930

With the nice weather finally with us I thought you might be interested in the titles of a couple of new local history books that will make great reading as you relax out in the backyard or on the chaise lounge up at the cottage. First, however, I must point out that since both have been self-published they will not be available at your local book store. Nevertheless, each makes for great reading and I have included details on how you can purchase a copy.

The first, *Street Stories of Toronto*, is by Herb Franklin and is a delightful account of his early years growing up in the area in and around Dovercourt Public School. If you lived in the Bloor, Ossington, Geary, Dufferin part of town this book's stories about local movie houses, neighbourhood bullies, corner stores, and trips to the Ex or Sunnyside will bring back a flood of memories. And even if you didn't, Herb's book makes for great reading. Of particular interest to me is the chapter on Dave White's sheet metal shop at the southeast corner of Dupont and Westmoreland where Herb worked during the summers of 1947 and 1948. One day in 1947 in walked local inventor Norman Breakey, who presented Dave with the working drawings for his latest invention. Dave proceeded to fabricate the first "Koton Kotor" for Breakey, who then presented it to the buyers down at Eaton's. And while it's claimed that Breakey never made money on his invention somebody sure did because today Breakey's paint roller/tray combination is sold all over the world.

Another suggestion is specifically aimed at those who are lucky enough to summer in the Barrie area. The East Georgian Bay Historical Foundation has recently reprinted its book *Barrie: A Nineteenth Century*

"KOTON KOTER"

ROLLS ON

PAINT

Smoothly glowing walls and woodwork, with the "Koton Koter Set" . . . designed to roll on oil or water paint. The covering is specially made from bias-cut cloth, replaceable when worn . . . the shaft of roller operates easily on a metal bearing. Set includes roller and box to hold the paint **1.98**

New covered cylinder to replace roller, each .... **.69**

THE PAINT DEPARTMENT ALSO SELLS

Products by the following manufacturers:

SCARFE PRODUCTS   GLIDDENS   BENJAMIN MOORE
FLO GLAZE   LOWE BROTHERS   SHERWIN WILLIAMS
C. I. L.   ACME

A 1946 newspaper ad for Toronto inventor Herb Breakey's revolutionary "Koton Kotor" available at Eaton's for $1.98.

Town. Packed with more than one hundred rare old photos, this book, which is available from the Foundation, c/o P.O. Box 518, Elmvale, ON. L0L 1P0 for $31.03 (tax and postage included), will enhance any visit to or stay in that pretty little city on the shores of Lake Simcoe.

LANDMARK CN TOWER TURNS 20

June 23, 1996

H ere's another of those "where has the time gone" stories. Would you believe that next Wednesday Toronto's very own CN Tower will be twenty years old? That's twenty!! It was on June 26, 1976 that the tower officially opened to the public. To celebrate the passing of two decades (makes the place sound even older, doesn't it?) the people at the tower are holding a community barbecue in nearby Bobby Rosenfeld Park from 11 am until 2:30 pm. Featured guests will be the fellows from *Forever Plaid.* The $5-per-person "donation" will be passed on to Operation Herbie at the Hospital for Sick Children. On that same day visitors to the tower who are twenty years old or have been

Model of the proposed Metropolitan Centre and the original version of Toronto's new communications tower, 1969.

married for twenty years will be admitted to the observation decks free. (Proof of age/marriage certificate required.) In addition, every fan attending that evening's Blue Jay game will receive a complimentary pass to the tower's observation deck.

The idea of a communications tower gracing the city's skyline was first noted in a 1967 proposal identified as Metropolitan Centre, a term later modified to simply Metro Centre. This massive 185-acre real estate development was to encompass all of the rail lands stretching across the city's waterfront between Bathurst and Yonge streets. Included in the Metropolitan Centre would be a new transportation centre that would replace Union Station, and a $50-million postal centre, and a 1,500–1,800 room convention hotel. A fourth component of the proposal was to be a, so-called, broadcasting centre, complete with a 1,500-foot tower that, as the proposal document described, would be made available to radio and TV stations, the police department, and both Canadian National and Canadian Pacific for all their telecommunications requirements. At this time, the tower was without a name, but because it was anticipated that the CBC would finally consolidate facilities scattered all over the city and move to the broadcasting centre it was a natural belief that it would become the CBC Tower. One additional feature of the proposed tower would be an observation deck at the 1,200-foot level, a vantage point described as being twice as high as the city's then tallest skyscraper the Toronto-Dominion Centre.

Frequently it is the case with mind-boggling megaprojects that miles and miles of political red tape eventually chokes them to death. So it was with Metro Centre, and in 1975 promoters reluctantly shelved the plan. But not before the communications tower component, now identified as the CN Tower, was well on its way to its ultimate cloud-piercing 553.3 metre (1,815' 5") height. In fact, it was on March 30 of that year that one of the most spectacular events in the tower's dizzying climb into the sky occurred when "Olga," a Sikorsky Skycrane helicopter hovering like a gigantic dragonfly, topped off the tower by placing the last of the thirty-six pieces that made up the tower's antenna mast. A little more than a year later the doors were opened to an attraction that now welcomes more than 1.7 million visitors annually.

The redesigned tower on its way up, September, 1973.

"Olga" tops off the new CN Tower on March 30, 1975.

CRAZY 'BOUT MY CLASSIC AUTOMOBILE

July 7, 1996

L ast week I related the fascinating story behind the birth of the Toronto-built Russell automobile and the successful effort by Betty Russell Anderson, daughter of the car's creator, to keep one of the last of these unique vehicles here in Canada. Beautifully restored, the 1914 model was reintroduced to admiring crowds at the conclusion of the Corel Great Race last weekend in Yorkville.

I know the pride Betty must have experienced as she took possession of her new/old car because as of three weeks ago I too became the proud owner of a vintage automobile. My story, though not as steeped in Canadian transportation history as Betty's, is, for me at least, just as exciting. Why? Well, it seems that at some point just hours before I got married nearly twenty-eight years ago I mentioned in an offhanded way "well, there goes my turquoise and white 1955 Pontiac," the car I had coveted ever since being enrolled in class 9B at North Toronto Collegiate that momentous day in September, 1955. In fact, it was the very thought of one day getting a turquoise and white 1955 Pontiac that made continuing my education at all relevant.

My beautifully restored 1955 Pontiac Laurentian looks pretty good alongside the TTC's beautifully restored 1923 Peter Witt streetcar. Lighthouse loop, June 15, 1996.

The wedding day came and went, as did another twenty-seven years, eight months, and twenty-one days (but who's counting?). Then, while entertaining a few friends one Saturday early this past June, my wife asked me to come to the front door for a minute. Someone selling something, I thought. Since the garage was in that direction anyway, I grabbed a bag of garbage on the way. I opened the front door and there in the driveway, surrounded by people I hadn't seen in months — years even — was a gleaming turquoise and white 1955 Pontiac Laurentian hardtop. The fact it was an Oshawa-built car was an important feature considering what I do for a living.

Seems that Yarmila had heard my comment and had originally intended surprising me with my dream car on my fiftieth birthday a few years ago. However, finding that precise make, model and colour combination wasn't easy. Yarmila enlisted the help of Dean Renwick, an old car expert (the term "old" goes with "car") who helped me stage a couple of vintage auto shows during my time working at the Ex. It took them more than four years to find "my" car, the one that magically appeared in the driveway that unforgettable Saturday night in June. Was I surprised? Is Lincoln a car?

* * * * *

The 1955 model year Pontiac was introduced to an amazed Toronto public on October 29, 1954. Its design was a major departure from all previous models, just as the Chevies, Fords, Chryslers, Cadillacs, and so on bore no resemblance to the 1954 models. While those goofy fins were still a few years in the future, the '55 models were unique, dripping chrome everywhere.

Back then new car models were literally kept under wraps until introduction day. In fact, so secret was the new Pontiac, the *Telegram's* new car reporter couldn't take it out on the streets to do his story, but was forced to perform his test drive on the roof of the City Buick-Pontiac building on Danforth Avenue.

Finally, on Thursday, October 28, full-page ads filled the dailies trumpeting the imminent arrival of the "all new from the ground up" Pontiacs. The descriptive text around the drawings of the various models would bring tears of joy to any marketing genius, even those of today. Expressions such as "all-new Glamoramic interiors" and "all-new wrap around panoramic," "4-fender visibility" and "4-way balanced ride," "tubeless tires" and "Strato-Streak V-8 engine" were chosen in hopes that people would beat down the dealers' doors the very next day just to get a closer look at these new cars. National Motors Limited, 945 Bay Street at Wellesley, went a step further, announcing that you could become a proud owner of a brand-new 1955 Pontiac for as little as $2,139.

Now, before you think that price was a real steal, in that same edition of the paper Dominion Store was advertising prime rib roast at 49¢ a pound. On the movie page admission to *The Caine Mutiny* at Shea's on Bay Street was $1 if you went after 6 pm. To get to that movie transit users paid 15¢ for an adult cash fare. Incidentally, the Yonge subway, all $67 million worth, was still in its first year of operation. Getting a jump on winter, Goodyear advertised a pair of 670 x 15 winter tires on sale for $28.90 and Canadian Tire offered motorists an automobile backup light kit (an option on Pontiac back then) for $1.79. Seat belts were still well in the future even as an option.

By the way, if you see me in my turquoise and white Pontiac at the local A&W having a Poppaburger please don't park too close. Thanks.

Cover of the dealer's catalogue for the 1955 model Pontiac.

THIS HOTEL WAS WITHOUT PEER

July 14, 1996

A 900-room hotel, to cost more than $10 million, will be built in the downtown area of Toronto it was learned today. It would be the second plan for a major downtown hotel advanced since Mayor Phillips made his appeal for increased accommodation last January. Complete details will not be released until the mayor makes an official announcement.

So wrote *Telegram* staff reporter William Bragg in the September 22, 1955 edition of the paper. That announcement by Nathan Phillips was not long in coming, for in the late edition of the same day's paper under the banner BULLETIN, it was revealed that an eighteen-storey structure to be called the Lord Simcoe Hotel would be erected on the northeast corner of King Street and University Avenue. Financing for the $9.5-million project would be from Toronto and Montreal sources. Then, as a kind of afterthought, the bulletin went on to state that the proposed building would be of steel construction, fireproof, and would have reinforced concrete floors.

When the official ground breaking took place later that year with Ontario Premier Leslie Frost on the end of the shovel, several things about Toronto's new hotel had changed. One was that it had grown a floor (it would now be nineteen instead of the original eighteen), while at the same time losing fifty rooms (it would now have 850, not 900 as first announced). Somehow this translated into a structure that would now only cost $9.5 million. But the most interesting change, historically at least, would come about if and when the premier's plea was answered. Phillips insisted that the name Lord Simcoe be altered to Governor Simcoe, since the province's first lieutenant-governor had never been elevated to the peerage. Seems Simcoe was never a lord! Should'a been, perhaps, but never was.

Recognizing the discrepancy, the owners sympathized but stuck with the name, pointing out that there was a Governor Simcoe Hotel already in Simcoe, Ontario. Besides, Lord Simcoe would undoubtedly look better on the letterhead, since the Simcoe's management company also managed the Lord Elgin up in Ottawa and the Lord Beaverbrook in Fredericton, New Brunswick.

With that minor historical irregularity out of the way work proceeded and on May 15, 1957 the new twenty-storey Lord Simcoe Hotel (it had gained another floor somewhere along the way, plus another half-million dollars in construction costs) was officially opened. Its nine hundred rooms, all with radios and television (Toronto's one and only TV station had been on the air for five years), were available at rates ranging from $8 for a single to $14 for a double. The hotel also boasted the Beau Nash cocktail lounge (later the Sentry Box Bar), the Captain's Table dining room and the Pump Room, which was a duplicate of the famous Pump Room in Chicago's Ambassador Hotel. It was in the Simcoe's Pump Room that *Telegram* restaurant critic Ron Evans experienced "a most impressive dinner for 2" even though the bill came to whopping nineteen bucks! Oh, the year of Ron's review? 1960.

As the years went by numerous financial setbacks befell the once-proud hotel and on June 29, 1979, less than twenty-three years after the hotel first opened, a small item on the business page announced that the hotel would be closed and the property sold. The end came on October 28, 1979. Before long there was no trace of the Simcoe. Historians' revenge?

In 1984 the sparkling corporate headquarters of the Sun Life Assurance Company of Canada opened on the site once occupied by the Lord Simcoe Hotel.

Builder's photo dated March 14, 1957 shows the Lord Simcoe Hotel nearing completion.

This 1996 photo taken by Alana Maksymiw shows the east tower of the new Sun Life Centre straddling the same University/King corner.

ON THE SUNNYSIDE OF THE BEACH

July 21, 1996

It was one of those perfect summer days: no humidity, clear as a bell, perfect picture taking weather. So I decided to visit Sunnyside. With a reprint of my 1982 book *I Remember Sunnyside* scheduled for this fall, I thought this would be the perfect time to update my collection of present-day views of the park. Armed with my trusty camera and a bunch of old views of the park, off I went.

Sunnyside, the area along Lake Ontario east of the Humber River, has been a popular people place for more than a century. Photographs taken a hundred or more years ago show Torontonians sunbathing on Sunnyside's original narrow beach, paddling in the waters of the old Humber Bay, or strolling along the wooden sidewalks in front of Pauline Meyer's restaurant where Sunday fish dinners were a specialty. Sunnyside's popularity increased dramatically following the opening of an amusement park in 1922. Built by the Toronto Harbour Commission as part of a huge waterfront redevelopment scheme, the park reached the pinnacle of fame and prominence during the Second World War when gasoline and tire rationing

The Bathing Pavilion today.

The new Sunnyside Bathing Pavilion, 1922

Sunnyside Amusement Park, 1929. Note the old railway station under the Turret cigarette sign and the elevator opening at trackside.

forced Torontonians to seek leisure-time pleasures close to home.

Bathing beauty contests, rides on the Derby Racer, Flyer, Bug, Whip, or Toboggan Wheel, a game of Tom Thumb golf, a ride on the ponies, a few minutes to see into the future with the palmist, a concert in front of the Orthophonic, a red hot and drink at the Honey Dew booth, a couple of

The same view today. Note the concrete outline of the old elevator entrance above the truck.

Downeyflake donuts … all this and more — that was Sunnyside. It all ended in 1955 when the rides and buildings came tumbling down. The new Metropolitan Toronto was too slick and fast-growing to have an old-fashioned amusement park on its doorstep.

During my visit I discovered that someone's trying to breathe a little life into the 1922 Sunnyside Bathing Pavilion with the opening of a restaurant in its picturesque courtyard. I wish them well.

In 1996 Dundurn Press reprinted my book *I Remember Sunnyside*, which first appeared back in 1982. Since it went out-of-print several years ago, I continued to receive more requests for a copy of this book than any other I've written. Thanks to Dundurn Press the book is now available in revised form complete with additional old photographs and newly researched text.

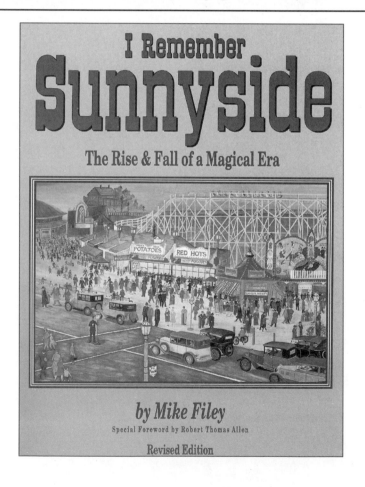

I Remember Sunnyside
The Rise & Fall of a Magical Era
by Mike Filey
Special Foreword by Robert Thomas Allen
Revised Edition

CELEBRATING TWO HUNDRED YEARS YONGE

July 28, 1996

On August 3 and 4 a special salute to Yonge Street's two-hundredth anniversary will be presented by the East Gwillimbury 200 Years Yonge Committee at Anchor Park in historic Holland Landing. This weekend of "living history" will feature more than 150 costumed participants representing regiments, militia groups and plain, ordinary townsfolk from those far-off days when Governor John Graves Simcoe, who had ordered Yonge Street built as a military road, was in charge. There'll also be period music, artillery demonstrations, a mock battle, and demonstrations of pioneer skills performed by local residents. As a special attraction the artifacts from the cornerstone of Holland Landing's Christ Church on the Hill, an 1843 creation of Toronto architect (and "warden" of High Park) John George Howard, will be on view to the general public for the first time. Call 1-905-478-2542 for details. A historic aside, the Town of East Gwillimbury is a proud community a few kilometres north of Metro and was named in honour of Governor Simcoe's wife, the former Elizabeth Posthuma (her mother died giving birth) Gwillim.

While on the subject of Yonge Street, it was a little more than fifty years ago that Fran Deck opened the second of his Toronto restaurants at 2275 Yonge Street, just steps north of the still rather sleepy Eglinton Avenue corner. Across from his new restaurant, Ernie Lick was trying to sell a few rusted-out Maxwells and Model A's from his used car lot. And if you bought one from Ernie and you needed some gas, there was the little Joy Oil station disguised as a miniature castle up at the Orchard View corner. Next door to Fran's, to the south, were branches of the Dominion Bank (it wouldn't join with the Bank of Toronto for another decade), Highland Dairy, and Ernest Axford's drug store with its windows full of perfumes, Thermogene, and cotton batten. To the north was the office of something called Lalla Motor Sales, Evelyne's Hat Shop, Margaret's Beauty Salon, and an electrical repair shop specializing in record players and replacement needles. (Remember when needles were used to create noise, not deaden it?) The locale was like a little town, except for out front when every few minutes one of those heavy Yonge streetcars pulling a trailer rumbled by. (Some of Fran's earliest customers were TTC

Yonge Street looking south to Eglinton Avenue, November, 1945. A sign in the window of the building to the extreme left of the photo announces the imminent opening of a new Fran's restaurant. Photo from the TTC Archives

Same view, a little more than half-a-century later.

crews from the old Eglinton car barn just down and across the street, right where the Eglinton subway station and towering office building are located.)

This north Yonge Street location was actually Francis Deck's second Toronto restaurant. Five years earlier the young man and his wife Ellen had moved to the city from Buffalo, New York where he had been managing some of the out-of-town branches of the Deck family's popular Decko chain of restaurants. Here in Toronto Deck opened a ten-seat eatery on the south side of St. Clair just west of Yonge and christened it with the colloquial form of his given name. "Fran's" was born. Incidentally, the St. Clair Avenue site, in a much expanded form, is still very much in business. Over the years other locations opened. With the recent move of the Yonge/Eglinton Fran's to a new location around the corner at 45 Eglinton Avenue East, there is, for the first time in more than half-a-century there is no Fran's restaurant on Yonge Street.

HERE'S WHERE YONGE ENDED TWO HUNDRED YEARS AGO

August 11, 1996

By now I'm sure just about everyone is aware that our very own Yonge Street is celebrating its two-hundredth anniversary this year. All the major local newspapers and many community papers, along with local radio and television stations have featured a number of stories about the pioneer thoroughfare that was born exactly two centuries ago.

As a result, we all now know that it was Governor Simcoe's intention to make Yonge a combination military/commercial highway connecting York with the British forts on the upper lakes and the riches of the northern forests and waterways. We also know that he named it in honour of his friend Sir George Yonge and that the road was slashed through the virgin forest

Holland Landing resident Jaime-Lynn Pizans and her dog Shadow survey the site where the original Yonge Street meets the Holland River.

surrounding York (now Toronto) by Simcoe's Rangers and that it was in early 1796 that they completed their work. So far, so good. But when it comes to Rainy River being part of the festivities, we stray from historical accuracy. Yonge Street's bicentennial has absolutely nothing to do with Rainy River, the modern-day terminus of the thoroughfare.

Rather, it has everything to do with the Town of East Gwillimbury and more precisely the Village of Holland Landing, which was the original northern terminus of Yonge Street two hundred years ago. Unfortunately, that fact seems to have eluded Toronto officials who failed to even invite East Gwillimbury officials to the kick-off ceremony for Yonge Street's two-hundredth earlier in the year. They opted to recognize Rainy River instead.

Well, as nice as the people from Rainy River no doubt, are Yonge Street's link with that community didn't come about until a relatively short thirty-one years ago when, on June 28, 1965, Ontario Premier John Robarts officially opened the stretch of Highway 11 between Fort Frances and Atikoken. As the Fort Frances — Rainy River section was already in place, as was the Atikoken — Thunder Bay connection, it was actually that 1965 event that finally connected Rainy River with provincial communities to the east and with Toronto at the other end of Highway 11 some 1,178.3 miles to the east and south.

To be historically accurate what we should be celebrating this year is the link established between Toronto and Holland Landing, a pretty community just north of Newmarket. It was on February 16, 1796 that surveyor Augustus Jones and the Rangers arrived at the bank of a river (named in recognition of the surveyor-general of the day, Samuel Holland) to complete the construction of the land portion of Simcoe's planned route to the upper lakes. Looking at a modern-day map the choice of that particular route becomes obvious. From Yonge Street's junction with the Holland River, exactly thirty-four miles and fifty-three chains north of the Lake Ontario shoreline, it's possible to use lakes Simcoe and Couchiching and the Severn River system (plus a few portages) to get to and from Lake Huron. Travel by water was much easier than trying to move troops or goods overland via a narrow trail blazed through the suffocating forest — surely an apt description of the Yonge Street created by the Rangers two centuries ago.

Several years went by and eventually a small community took root on the banks of the river not far from where Simcoe's Rangers laid down their axes. In the beginning it was known as St. Albans, then as Beverley before being renamed Holland Landing in 1821. Several years ago, Holland Landing became part of the sprawling Town of East Gwillimbury. That town also has an interesting connection with Governor Simcoe. Elizabeth, his wife, was born Elizabeth Gwillim, and it is from her that the town takes its current name.

Happy two-hundredth Yonge Street, to the Toronto–Holland Landing section at least.

* * * * *

Here's another piece of Yonge Street trivia. Ever notice the bend in Yonge Street just north of St. Clair Avenue? It's there, but most people are too busy keeping their eyes on the traffic to notice. Retired land surveyor Bill Gates (the other one) was good enough to explain to me that this deviation was no doubt simply a re-alignment of the street after it was first laid out two hundred years ago. Unlike the surveyors of today who have exotic instruments and satellites to work with, the pioneer surveyors had to rely on simple compasses and heavy Gunter's chains in their quest to lay out a road system through the forests. Inaccuracies frequently crept in and alterations would subsequently be made, as was the case with the realignment of Yonge Street north of the 3rd Concession Road (today's St. Clair Avenue).

The bend in Yonge Street north of St. Clair is clearly visible in this photo taken from the top of the CFRB building.

THESE WALLS PICTURE OUR PAST

August 18, 1996

Created by artist John Hood in 1993 as a tribute to Toronto's two-hundredth anniversary (the city having been established in 1793 as the Town of York, a name bestowed on it by Lieutenant-Governor Simcoe on August 27 of that year), the huge mural on the south wall (Front Street East) of the *Sun* Building has become one of Toronto's most entertaining — and educational — tourist attractions. Every day bus loads of visitors to our city scrutinize the 160-foot-long panorama that graphically presents many of the people and events from our city's fascinating past. Visitors to the mural, be they tourists from all corners of the earth or merely Torontonians eager to learn about the city's past, are encouraged to pick up a free copy of a guide to the mural available from specially marked *Sun* newspaper boxes nearby.

Wall murals in various styles, some of an advertising nature, others, wildly artistic and a few, like John's, graphic "blasts from the past," can be found all over Metro. Many representatives of the latter category are visible on the sides of structures along Kingston Road. This project was initiated by the Scarborough Arts Council and funded through grants from various levels of government as well as private donations. Collectively titled Mural Roots, the first of this collection, which now totals ten, was also created by *Sun* muralist John Hood. His 1990 work, titled "Halfway House," can be found at 2502 Kingston Road (on the north side, a few steps west of Midland Ave.). The most recent addition to the Mural Roots series was unveiled earlier this summer at 2835 Kingston Road (south side at St. Clair Avenue and opposite the Canadian Tire store). It's the work of Jennifer and Phil Richards who live in the nearby Cliffcrest community, and is titled "In the Way of Progress." The scene depicts the Kingston Road/St. Clair Avenue intersection as it may have appeared one bright spring day back in 1922. The flow of rush hour traffic, such as it was in those days, is delayed by a rather apathetic cow — of the Holstein variety I believe — who has wandered away from the nearby farmer's field. (Boy, I hope it is a Holstein or the Royal Winter Fair's new boss, Dave Garrick, won't let me hear the end of it. That's assuming, of course, that he knows what it is.)

"In the Way of Progress", the tenth and most recent mural in the Mural Roots collection, can be seen on the wall of the Stop 17 variety store at 2835 Kingston Road.

A "real life" photo of a radial car similar to #213 Westbound in front of the Halfway House, Kingston Road and Midland Avenue, c.1918.

Of particular interest in the view is car #213, which was built for the Toronto and York (T&Y) Radial Railway Company in 1909. This type of vehicle was known as a radial car because it was part of a project championed by the father of Ontario Hydro, Sir Adam Beck, who foresaw high speed electric commuter/freight lines radiating out from Toronto. Interestingly, the term radial was purely a local euphemism. Elsewhere, especially south of the border where this type of service was extremely prevalent, they were referred to as interurban cars.

In the mural passengers board car #213 Westbound at Stop 17 (St. Clair Avenue). The new Scarborough High School (later renamed R.H. King to honour the school's first principal) looms in the left background.

The Scarborough radial line was one of three operated by the T&Y, the others being Mimico (from the city limits to Port Credit via the Lakeshore Road) and the Metropolitan (from the city limits north on Yonge Street to Aurora then cross-country to Jackson's Point on Lake Simcoe and Sutton).

The Scarborough cars connected with the city streetcars at the east limits and eventually ran as far east as West Hill. In 1922 the line was turned over to the City of Toronto and operated by the Hydro Electric Power Commission of Ontario (now Ontario Hydro). Five years later the line became part of the expanding TTC operations, only to have the familiar green radial cars replaced by buses in 1936.

*   *   *   *   *

The Scarborough Arts Council has prepared posters (@ $20), limited edition prints (@$100) and T-shirts ($15) all featuring the view captured in this marvellous mural. Call (416) 698-7322 for ordering details and for further information on the Mural Roots project.

A CENTURY OF CINEMA

August 25, 1996

Whether its a quick jaunt around the corner to the friendly neighbourhood theatre or an excursion to one of the modern multi-screen cinemas located in a sprawling mall, going to the show remains a popular pastime for many of us.

As a kid my favourite haunts included the Alhambra, Midtown, and Metro on Bloor Street West. When we moved to north Toronto the favourites became the Circle and Capital on Yonge Street and Belsize, and Mt. Pleasant on Mt. Pleasant Road. Sure there were other theatres nearby — the International Cinema, Odeon Fairlawn, Eglinton — but they were slightly more high class (read expensive) and so I seldom saw the insides of those places.

Every once in a while when a special movie arrived in Toronto our family would head off to one of the big downtown movie houses such as the Loew's or Victoria. The former remains as the Elgin; the latter is just a memory. I especially remember seeing *Bambi* at the Tivoli, a giant of a picture palace that was located at the southeast* corner of Victoria and Richmond, just along the street from the Victoria.

Over the years several Torontonians have shared the names of their favourite movie houses with me. Let's see if I can remember some of them. Oh yeah, Cum-C and Cum-Bak (great names), the Prince of Wales, Kent, Palace, Joy, Blue Bell, Colonial, Hippodrome, Imperial, Rio, Biltmore, Uptown, and so on. I could fill a whole page with their names.

Historically, the year 1996 marks the one-hundredth anniversary of going to the movies here in Toronto. To be precise, it all started a century ago next Saturday (August 31, 1896) when an entrepreneur from Buffalo, New York, one M.S. Robinson, opened his Musee in a small store at 81 Yonge Street, on the east side a few steps north of King Street, in the very heart of the young city.

Robinson invited Torontonians to buy a 10¢ ticket, enter a darkened room, and view the latest marvel of the age, inventor Thomas Edison's new

---

* See September 8, 1996 column.

In this c.1895 view showing the east side of Yonge Street, J.H. Moore's Theatre and Musee, the forerunner of Robinson's Musee, can be seen in the middle of the block. Note the then-new Confederation Life building at the Adelaide Street corner in the background.

Vitascope machine flashing life-like moving pictures on a white painted wall. Before long crowds were lining up to see the latest marvel of the age.

Actually, Edison's Vitascope had received its public introduction several months earlier in New York City. It was such a success that before long similar machines were projecting all kinds of short films on makeshift screens in vaudeville houses all over the States.

Robinson chose August 31 as the date for the machine's Toronto premiere, knowing full well that on the following day, September 1, a competing form of moving picture machine developed by France's Lumiere brothers was scheduled to be introduced to the visitors at the 1896 edition of the Toronto Industrial Exhibition (a Toronto tradition that was to be renamed the Canadian National Exhibition a few years later).

Robinson took full advantage of the huge crowds who were in town eagerly anticipating the fair and ran newspaper ads trumpeting his Vitascope machine that was already up and running. And, just in case Edison's marvel wasn't enough to draw them in (Canadians being less excitable than Americans, perhaps) in the same building he also offered displays of mysterious X-rays (another new scientific marvel discovered in 1895 by German physicist Dr. Wilhelm Roentgen), an assortment of works of art, an animal menagerie, and musical selections performed by Hearon's Lady Orchestra.

Both the Robinson demonstration as well as the one put on by Exhibition officials were unqualified financial successes. But moving pictures remained just a novelty until both projection equipment and selection of movies had improved sufficiently to turn that novelty into a business with an unlimited future.

In early 1906, recognizing an opportunity to get in on the ground floor, Toronto-born circus man John Griffin had the distinction of opening Canada's first permanent movie theatre. He did it by simply emptying out a store on the east side of Yonge just north of Queen (almost next door to today's Elgin theatre), thereby turning it into a small auditorium. He painted a large white rectangle on one wall, and installed several rows of wooden chairs and one of the new-fangled projectors. He called the country's first movie house the Theatorium. In a nice twist of Canadiana (purely by accident, I'm sure), one of the first films shown in his Theatorium featured May Irwin from Whitby, Ontario.

In honour of the centennial of the first moving picture to be shown in Toronto, the Toronto Historical Board and the Toronto Film Society will unveil a commemorative plaque in the courtyard of 1 Financial Place (southeast corner of Yonge and Adelaide streets), just steps from the site of Robinson's Musee, on Wednesday, August 28 at 4 pm, to which the public is invited.

Happy Seventy-Fifth, TTC

September 1, 1996

Okay, here's a little Toronto trivia appropriate for this special day. Who was Robert Ferguson and why is he important in the annals of public transportation history here in the great city of Toronto? And for the second part of this question, what was his home address and where was he employed?

Don't know?

Time's up!

Actually, I didn't expect that anyone would know the answers to the questions (I sure didn't 'til I read the newspaper), but Mr. Ferguson really is a part of our city's history because he was the very first paying passenger on the streetcars of the brand new Toronto Transportation Commission that went into business exactly seventy-five years ago this very day.

TTC guides assist passengers boarding a *Bloor* PCC car in early 1950. Note the car card advertising singer Frankie Lane's March 10 appearance at the Arena on Mutual Street.

Mayor Robert Saunders cuts the obligatory ribbon as the Lansdowne trolley coach goes into service June 19, 1947.

And how do I know that? Well, in the *Evening Telegram* of September 1, 1921 it's reported that one Robert Ferguson of 285 Brunswick Avenue, an employee of the King Edward Hotel, boarded a *Belt Line*-route streetcar westbound on King Street just as the trio of bells in the City Hall tower ceased their midnight peeling and the month of August, 1921 became history.

And just as today's TTC is frequently the subject of criticism, the fledgling commission of seventy-five years ago was also faced with its detractors. In fact, the new municipally run service wasn't even a day old and the papers began agitating for a return to the good old days of private operation when the adult fare was only a nickel. The new service had bumped the fare forty percent to 7¢ cash. That was bad enough, but what compounded the problem was the fact that on that first day the new books of fifty tickets for (which sold for $3.00, making the new fare a slightly more acceptable 6¢) were virtually unavailable. Thousands walked or took to their bikes rather than paying that extra cent. Right then and there many vowed never to return to the transit vehicles. Another problem arose that first day as a good number of streetcars ran well behind schedule as conductors were forced to make change or watch as irate passengers dropped seven pennies in the fare box, one coin at a time. All in all that first day, three-quarters-of-a-century ago, was a public relations flop.

And yet the concept of a transit service run for the benefit of the public was seen as a giant step forward in a city where, except for a brief period in the early 1890s, the travelling public had been held hostage by private entrepreneurs who were more intent on making money than providing a reliable and efficient transit service. In several cases, in an effort to serve those outlying areas of the sprawling city that had been forsaken by the private interests because of limited ridership, the city was forced to build a progression of short streetcar lines that connected with the city system. But it was still necessary for these suburban riders to pay an extra fare.

From the initiation of horsecar operation in 1861 through the electrification of the system during the period 1892–94 and right up until 1921, a clutch of transportation czars kept a stranglehold on Torontonians' ability to travel in and around their fast-growing community.

On a couple of occasions minor attempts were made to wrestle control of the streetcars away from people like Messrs. Everett, Kiely, Fleming, and Mackenzie, but it wasn't until the municipal election of 1920 that a clear mandate was given by a frustrated electorate to get on with bringing all public transportation in the city under municipal control. The enabling provincial legislation took effect on September 1, 1921. On that first day a total of 544,000 people rode the system. Some grumbled while others praised the long overdue change.

Over the intervening seven-and-a-half decades the TTC, like any municipal (or private for that matter) operation, has had its ups and downs. Unfortunately, when things are up nothing is said, but when they're down … look out.

Happy seventy-fifth, TTC. Metro Toronto is a great place to live thanks in great measure to you and all your fine people.

A more complete history of the TTC is covered in my new book, *The TTC Story: the First Seventy-five Years, published* in 1996 by Dundurn Press.

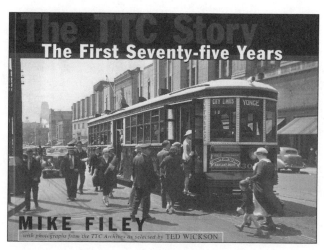

And on this Corner...

September 8, 1996

Shea's Victoria (1910–1952). Photo courtesy City of Toronto Archives.

O kay! Okay! I admit it. I made a mistake in my column of a couple of weeks back. But, what the heck, one slip-up in more than twenty years of churning out this stuff ain't bad.

What's that?

Well, maybe there has been more than just one goof, however all the others were the work of those ubiquitous writers' gremlins. This one was all mine.

* * * * *

In the August 25 column I described the centennial of motion pictures here in Toronto, and a few eagle-eyed readers caught my incorrect placement of the Tivoli Theatre at the southeast corner of Victoria and Richmond streets in downtown Toronto. Well, I'm here to set the record straight. The Tivoli was located on the southwest corner; Shea's Victoria was on the southeast.

The Tivoli (originally the Allen, 1917–1964) as it looked in 1927.

Actually, my slip is almost forgivable since this pair of movie palaces stood directly opposite each other in the heart of the busy city for almost four decades. I'm sure that even long-time movie goers frequently entered the wrong building by mistake.

The older of these two theatres, Shea's Victoria, opened on August 1, 1910 and was the creation of Mike and Jerry Shea, entertainment entrepreneurs from Buffalo, New York. Recognizing that the bustling City of Toronto was a perfect market for a new vaudeville and moving-picture house, the boys had opened their first Toronto property in 1899 at 81 Yonge Street. Interestingly this theatre called, not surprisingly, Shea's, was located in the same building in which Torontonians had witnessed for the very first time the newest wonder of the age, moving pictures. As described in my August 25 column (the part that was correct) that event occurred on Friday, August 31, 1896, exactly a century ago. A historic plaque was recently erected on the site by the Toronto Historical Board and the Toronto Film Society.

As the crowds grew larger the boys were forced to abandon their small Yonge Street theatre, moving into a new 1,800-seat playhouse they had built up the street and around the corner at the southeast quadrant of the Victoria/Richmond intersection. Shea's Victoria, described in the newspapers as being "the paragon of comfort and the acme of safety," opened on August 1, 1910 with a selection of vaudeville acts that included cyclists, singers, dancers, and a guy named William Ferry who was described as "the Human Frog," plus "selections from the kinetograph," an early version of the movie projector. Newspaper ads indicate the Victoria (as it became known) closed at the end of 1952 (*The Greatest Show on Earth* was the last movie), though the building wasn't demolished for another three years. The site remains a parking lot!!

In 1917, even as the Great War ravished Europe, the Allen brothers, founders of the once-great Allen chain of fifty or so theatres that stretched across Canada, opened their mammoth new 1,553-seat flagship theatre at 13 Richmond Street East, right across Victoria Street from Shea's. When Allen Theatres, Ltd. got into financial difficulties in 1923, Famous Players acquired the theatre and renamed it the Tivoli. The Tivoli remained in business until it closed on November 4, 1964. (A movie called *False Shame* was the last to illuminate the theatre's massive screen, which over the years had featured the first film with a soundtrack seen, and heard, in Toronto [*Street Angel*]; *The Jazz Singer* featuring former Toronto hotel bellboy Al Jolson; and the wonderful *Oklahoma!* in Todd-AO.) The new Cambridge Suites Hotel now stands on the site.

Got it? Shea's Victoria on the southeast corner, the Tivoli on the southwest. I hope I don't forget, again.

MAKING PLANS FOR THE FUTURE

September 15, 1996

So what's so unusual about going ahead with the building of a subway tunnel without making provision for either tracks or station structures? This certainly isn't the first time that transportation experts have proceeded with a project here in Toronto knowing full well that its real worth wouldn't be realized until sometime in the future. A perfect example of this foresightedness was the provision of a subway right-of-way under the new bridge being built over the Don Valley to connect Bloor Street with the Danforth district. Many are under the impression that it was Toronto Works Commissioner Roly Harris (who's remembered in the name of the R.C. Harris Filtration Plant on Queen Street East) who thought up the idea of incorporating the right-of-way under the massive structure. In fact, it was the well-known American transit consulting firm of Jacobs and Davies who, in their 1910 report on the future transportation requirements commissioned by Toronto City Council, foresaw the growth of the Danforth district and emphatically urged the incorporation of a tube right-of-way as part of the Bloor-Danforth viaduct. (Back then subways were still being called "tubes," while the term "subway" was used to describe a thoroughfare constructed under a set or sets of railway tracks.)

In this photo the west end of the Don Section of the Prince Edward Viaduct is under construction, and the opening under the main deck for a "tube" line is plainly visible. This provision would be used more than half-a-century later when the Bloor-Danforth subway line opened on February 26, 1966.

A second report prepared by another transportation expert, Bion J. Arnold of Chicago and released two years after the massive Jacobs and Davies chronicle, reiterated the importance of both the bridge and the right-of-way, although he saw the latter initially as a route for streetcars that would be upgraded to subway train operation if and when passenger traffic reached appropriate levels. Interestingly, this same argument is presently being used to promote a light rapid transit (streetcar) service on the Sheppard route that could be upgraded to a full subway if and when required.

When the entire $2.5-million, 5,287-foot-long structure opened in 1919, surface streetcars began running on the upper level while the lower right-of-way sat unused until trains on the new Bloor-Danforth commenced operating forty-seven years later. It took a while, but the consultants' foresight eventually paid off.

On the other hand, or drawing board, well-intentioned plans go awry. Take the "ghost" station on the proposed Queen subway line. This line, to be equipped with streetcars initially and upgraded to full subway operation when needed, was to be built once the Yonge line was complete. While that never happened the station was nevertheless "roughed in" when the Queen station on the Yonge line was built in 1949/50. Since there would be entrances at James Street the proposed station was identified in the reports as City Hall station ("old" City Hall sitting at the northwest corner of the Queen and James intersection).

Nearly eighty years after the formal opening, steelwork at the west end of the viaduct is again being cleaned (and repaired where necessary), coated, and painted. Eventually, all the steelwork on the 5,287-foot-long structure will be cleaned by Metro Toronto.

Here's another example of farsightedness falling short. In the fall of 1935 work began on the construction of a tunnel to the site of the city's proposed new airport at the west end of Toronto Island. A hole was actually started at the foot of Bathurst Street adjacent to the Western Entrance seawall. The government of the day up in Ottawa suddenly changed its mind and in late October, 1935 the hole was filled in and the project shelved. Guess what they're contemplating now? A tunnel to the Island. Get out the shovels.

And then there's the light rail platform at Kipling station, the western terminus of the Bloor-Danforth subway. It was constructed for the use of light rail transit vehicles that may someday shuttle passengers to and from Pearson International Airport. But don't hold your breath.

And what about the tunnel under Eglinton Avenue West? Enough already.

Housing the Forces that Provide Neighbourhood Protection

September 22, 1996

Recently my wife and I were invited to a special ceremony presented by the Order of St. John. Held in the magnificent Canadian Room of the Royal York Hotel, the event recognized a number of men and women who, by remarkable acts of bravery, had saved their fellow citizens from severe injury or even death, often at great personal risk to themselves.

We had the honour of being seated at a table with two Metro Toronto policemen, Constables Peter Moreira and Colin Sinclair, each of whom had recently received the St. John Ambulance Life Saving Award.

In Colin's case he had come to the aid of an individual who had been stabbed at a subway station. Using the first aid training given to all Metro police (as well as to all Metro area firefighters and TTC personnel) by St. John Ambulance, he was able to stabilize the victim until professional medical action arrived on the scene. Peter and his partner, Lawrence Walsh, prevented a psychiatric patient from committing suicide, even while the two young constables were being threatened themselves.

No. 4 Police Station/No. 7 Fire Hall, Dundas and Parliament streets, 1954.

During the course of the evening Peter mentioned something that made him an even more remarkable fellow than I first thought. As an avid *Sun* reader he told me that the first article he sought out in his Sunday paper was my column. (Or was his first choice Max Haines's column and mine was second?... No matter, he had said the magic words.)

His interest in history naturally resulted in our

Toronto's ancient Don Jail, the cornerstone of which was laid in 1859. While still under construction the building was destroyed by fire in 1862. Work soon resumed and the jail finally opened in 1864.

chatting about the early days of policing here in our city. Peter, who works out of 51 Division in the Regent Park part of downtown Toronto, related how he frequently hears stories from some old timers about the "good old days" in and around the Dundas Street East/Parliament Street neighbourhood. Most remembered, with mixed emotions, the predecessor to today's modern building that's home to Peter and the other personnel of 51 Division.

Known as No. 4, the distinctive structure was erected in 1870 on the north side of Dundas Street (then called Wilton Avenue) just east of the Parliament Street corner. To save some tax money it was a combination police and fire station with No. 7 fire hall occupying the east end of the structure. The building's lofty tower served as the site of a large neighbourhood timepiece, as well as being the place where hoses were hung to dry after running a fire.

The antiquated No. 4 station was closed at the end of 1955 and replaced by a new No. 4. The new station retained that title for just a short time, being renamed 51 Division in 1957. It was in this year that the various police departments in and around the City of Toronto were amalgamated under the Metro Police banner, with former Toronto chief John Chisholm as the new leader (or so he thought, but that's another story for another time).

The new $400,000 station, described by some as "the continent's most modern", was featured in a January 25, 1956 *Toronto Telegram* story. In it, some staff reporter named Douglas Creighton called the station a "dazzler."

While we're on the subject of landmark structures, I see the government has once again announced its intention to close the Don Jail. This time it's the 1958 addition to the original 1866 structure whose time is up. I wonder if this plan will take as long to implement as the original scheme to close the old jail? That closure was first suggested by Mayor Church at a meeting on January 9, 1919! But, he added, the only way to do that was to cut off supplies.

CATHEDRAL TO RING IN TWO HUNDRED YEARS

September 29, 1996

1997 will be one of special importance for Toronto's very own St. James' Cathedral, for in that year the congregation will celebrate its two-hundredth anniversary.

* * * * *

In 1797 Peter Russell, successor to John Simcoe, the founder of the Town of York (which was renamed Toronto when the community was given city status in 1834) decided to enlarge the townsite. This expansion would take place west of the original town plot, and the boundary of the addition would be a street now called Peter.

Recognizing the needs of the many Church of England adherents living in York, Russell also decreed that within that addition provision would be made for an Anglican church and graveyard. The parcel selected for this purpose comprised six acres of heavily wooded land bounded by today's King, Jarvis, Adelaide, and Church streets. In fact, it was because the land was being reserved for the church that the latter thoroughfare, the road that led to and from the church, became known as Church Street.

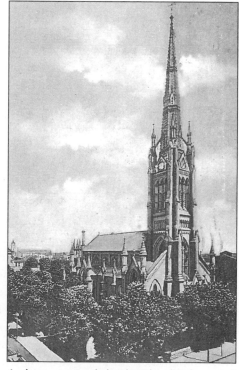

A picture postcard showing the church around the turn of the century.

Many years were to pass before a house of worship was erected on the site, and in the interim the fledgling congregation was offered meeting space in Government House, a small brick structure located on the water's edge just south and west of the present Parliament–King Street intersection. Because the parliament of the provincial government met in this building, the selection of the title Parliament Street for the road leading to the building becomes obvious.

Work finally began on erecting a proper house of worship in 1803. The site selected for the new church was at the southwest quadrant of the church plot. Following the removal of a large stand of pine trees and with the aid of the soldiers from the Garrison, a 50' x 40' wooden structure was constructed. For

One of the earliest photographs taken in Toronto shows the new bells for St. James' Cathedral being transported to the church c. 1865. Photo from the Baldwin Room, Metro Toronto Reference Library.

years it was known simply as the Church at York. The name St. James' wasn't adopted until 1828.

With the constant increase in population (and the resultant increase in the number of faithful followers) larger structures became necessary. In 1818 the original church was enlarged, then replaced by a brick building that opened in 1832. Seven years later this structure burned to the ground and a third church was built. When this one opened in 1840 it became home to the Bishop's "cathedra" or seat, and was consecrated as the city's first cathedral. In 1849 this building was also destroyed by flames.

In 1853 the present beautiful structure opened, but without its magnificent spire. It was added, along with a complement of nine bells, in 1865. The tower clock, a gift of the citizens of Toronto, was placed in the 174-foot-high spire (for many years the world's tallest) in 1875. A tenth bell was added in 1928 giving the cathedral what is known as an "American style" chime of fixed bells. These are played with swinging hammers and provide a clock chime and a miniature carillon.

In honour of the congregation's bicentennial, plans are underway to install a full ring of twelve bells, ten of which have pealed from the spire of St. James' Church in Bermondsey, England until acquired by our St. James'. Cast in 1829, these bells have rung through times of war and peace and soon, along with two additional bells to be cast at the historic Whitechapel Bell Foundry in London, they will ring out once again.

The present schedule anticipates that the bells will be moved to the church from the waterfront (just as the original nine were 131 years ago, although back then the trip was shorter) sometime around Easter, 1997. Watch this column for details. Once installed in the tower plans call for special concerts and even change-ringing lessons for the general public.

All of the money required to purchase and transport the bells, as well as to make the necessary modifications and additions to the cathedral spire, will come from sources other than the cathedral itself. An organization called the Bells of Old York has been established to raise the necessary funds. They eagerly seek your help. If you'd like more information write to Bells of Old York, 65 Church Street, Toronto M5C 2E9.

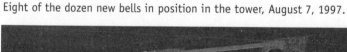

The new bells were installed in early 1997 and officially dedicated on June 27, 1997.

Eight of the dozen new bells in position in the tower, August 7, 1997.

Fields of Dreams

October 6, 1996

Several weeks ago I wrote about a few of the transportation projects of years gone by that only got as far as the proposal stage, never really fulfilling the planners' true expectations. The Queen subway "ghost" station, the Islington-Pearson International Airport LRT (Light Rail Transit) station, and the "on again–off again" tunnel under the Western Channel are prime examples.

Then I got to thinking about other dream projects that looked like sure winners only to be short-circuited soon after they were announced. Especially intriguing, with the construction of the new Air Canada Centre for the Raptor basketball team in some disarray, are the various sports stadia that appeared to be certainties until someone, somewhere, pulled the plug. Take, for instance, a thing called Civic Stadium that was proposed for the Exhibition grounds in 1917. It was to be just the ticket for all those hardball, soccer, and basketball (!!!) players and track and field athletes who were hampered by the lack of proper facilities. And it would be perfect for the Olympic Games the city was bound to get sooner or later. Obviously later.

While nothing happened right away — owing to just about everbody's preoccupation with the rather uncertain outcome of the Great War — the idea did get a kick-start once victory had been achieved. In fact, this time it was to be a War Memorial stadium dedicated to all those young Canadians who would never return home. The structure would seat 12,000 spectators and sit on the newly reclaimed waterfront somewhere between the Exhibition grounds and the proposed Sunnyside bathing beach and amusement park. Pretty drawings and working plans were prepared. The project seemed a certainty (after all, 40,000 city athletes were counting on it), but when the project was placed on the municipal ballot of January 1, 1923 it was soundly defeated. I can only assume that a lot of those eager athletes were too young to vote. Actually, the reason given for the project's defeat was that $225,000 was just too expensive.

The stadium idea just wouldn't go away, and the papers are full of other dreams like that of the amazing Jack Kent Cooke, owner of the Maple Leaf baseball team in the International League. If the major league officials would allow him entry into either the National of American league he would see to it that a proper big league stadium was built. And to emphasize his determination this composite photo (bottom of the page) was released. It's actually Chicago's Wrigley Field superimposed on an aerial view of Riverdale Flats. (That's Broadview Avenue between the Danforth and Gerrard Street in the background. Today the Don Valley Parkway roars through the site.) Cooke's dream never came true and a very disgruntled Jack moved to the States where he finally got his way, big time.

The list of sports-stadium sites proposed over the years would fill the rest of this page: the foot of Bathurst Street, Ramsden Park (north of Yonge and Davenport), Exhibition Place (there have been several suggested for this place, including a 1956 idea to build a 64,840-seat stadium for $6 million that would incorporate the old grandstand, which now appears to be on its last legs), Downsview Airport (what airplanes? what runway?), and the railway lands on the waterfront are just a few. And while none of these projects got off the drawing board, many years later SkyDome would open on the railway lands site.

Proposed Memorial Stadium, western waterfront version, 1922.

PROPOSED MEMORIAL STADIVM
FOR THE
CITY OF TORONTO

Proposed major league sports stadium, Don Valley version, 1954.

OUR BRIDGE TO LEASIDE

October 13, 1996

S everal weeks ago the federal government announced that the name of the new $900-million bridge connecting New Brunswick with Prince Edward Island will be "Confederation Bridge." Nice choice. But certainly not unique. In fact, I'll bet you didn't know that Toronto also has a bridge by that same name. Actually, I'm not surprised that most people don't know the whereabouts of our Confederation Bridge since it doesn't seem to have been called that since the structure opened almost seventy years ago.

* * * *

From the day it was incorporated, May 7, 1913, Leaside, with its burgeoning population of forty-three industrious souls, lay in virtual isolation far out in the country many miles from the City of Toronto. The origins of Leaside, and in fact of the name itself, go back much further — to 1881 to be precise — when the new CPR, working hard to gain rail access into Toronto, established a work depot in the Lea family orchards and honoured James, the father, by calling the place Leaside. Another railway company — the Canadian Northern — came along early in the new century and looked at developing Leaside into a true railway town. The Canadian Northern didn't survive, but the seeds of a new town did.

Improved access to Thorncliffe race track, which stood on a site now occupied by the East York Town Centre and adjacent apartment towers, was a major reason why a new bridge was so so necessary.

For years the only way to get to Leaside from Yonge Street was via one of the sideroads — Soudan, Merton, or Balliol — that were laid out specifically to provide access to the newly incorporated townsite. Once in the town the only houses were on Airdrie and Rumsey roads, the latter named in honour of

Reginald Rumsey, the bank inspector who kept an eye on how the town's money was being spent. Most of these dwellings were built by Canada Wire and Cable, a pioneer industry in Leaside with a huge factory on Laird Drive. Another early industry was the Durant Motor Company, whose fine cars went the way of the dodo. Nearby were the grass fields of the sprawling Leaside Airfield, while at the south end of town fans flocked to the popular Thorncliffe race track.

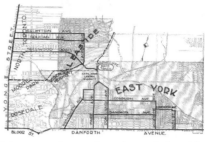

This map, from the souvenir booklet commemorating the opening of the Leaside Bridge (identified here as the East York-Leaside Viaduct) shows its location and importance in bringing those two communities (and Toronto) together

With all this activity it became painfully obvious that better access to and from the town was an absolute necessity. That access would come by way of a new bridge erected over the valley of the Don to connect Leaside on the north side of the valley with the community of Todmorden on the south. From there the city was just a bus and streetcar journey away. Work on the million-dollar structure began in late 1926. When the ceremonial ribbon was cut just 263 days later a new world's speed record for the construction of a structure of this size had been established. The bridge was officially dedicated on October 29, 1927 and proudly acclaimed as the Confederation Bridge (1927 being the sixtieth anniversary of the joining together of the original four provinces). Never a nation of flag wavers, we now refer to it simply as the Leaside Bridge. Pity!

It's hard to believe from this July 7, 1927 photo that the new bridge would be ready for traffic in less than four months. The strucure even came in at a figure $25,000 under budget.

Dedication plaque on the East York–Leaside Bridge, as the structure came to be known.

CELEBRATING SEVENTY-FIVE YEARS OF COMMUNITY SERVICE

October 20, 1996

You know, with all the gloom and doom concerning the future of various Metro area hospitals it's nice to be able to pass along a happy story concerning one of the city's busiest and most respected medical establishments. This year St. Joseph's Health Centre, on The Queensway just west of the busy King/Queen/Roncesvalles intersection, a city landmark that's still known to thousands simply as St. Joe's, a term used with respect and admiration, is proudly celebrating its seventy-fifth anniversary.

Actually, you can tell those who've been around for a while (I'm not looking at anyone in particular) because they continue to use the hospital's original name, St. Joseph's Hospital even though the "Health Centre" moniker came into effect sixteen years ago when St. Joe's merged with the nearby Our Lady of Mercy Hospital. It's like calling Danforth Avenue "the Danforth" or Pearson International Airport, "Malton." Colloquialisms like those simply identify long-time Torontonians. While the hospital, oops,

The Sister's of St. Joseph's original Sacred Heart Orphanage towers over John Howard's Sunnyside Villa. In 1922, the friendly sounds of the new Sunnyside amusement park down on the lakefront would begin wafting through the new St. Joseph's Hospital that had opened in these buildings the previous year.

St. Joseph's Health Centre today. The parking garage, erected in 1977, sits on the site of the old Sunnyside Villa.

health centre is celebrating seventy-five years of community service, the institution's origins in reality go back much further than the year 1921. In fact, we can trace those origins to the year 1851 when four Catholic Sisters of the Congregation of St. Joseph arrived in Toronto from Philadelphia in response to an urgent plea for help in administering to the needs of some of the city's many orphans. The sisters established an orphanage on Nelson (now Jarvis) Street just south of Queen. Unfortunately, the need for increased accommodation was always a problem and in 1859 the house at 100 Jarvis Street was vacated and the youngsters transferred to the rambling House of Providence on Power Street. Before many more years had passed the Sisters searched the city for even larger premises. Their prayers were answered in 1876 when they were offered the use of an old structure erected several decades earlier by John Howard on the eastern edge of his property, High Park. The house stood on the sunny side of a hill overlooking Humber Bay and was called, naturally enough, Sunnyside. It was to this quiet location well out in the western suburbs of the city that thirty-six infants from the House of Providence were relocated. In 1881 the Sisters of St. Joseph purchased Sunnyside and a few years later increased the number that could be accommodated by building an substantial addition, into which the boys were moved. It was at this time that the name Sunnyside was dropped in favour of Sacred Heart Orphanage. In 1891 a second addition was built, into which the girls from Power Street were relocated.

The work of administering to the needs of several hundred orphans continued at the Sunnyside location for the next couple of decades. Then, sometime in 1920, the Sisters began hearing rumours that the city fathers were investigating the possibility of expropriating part of the orphanage site in order to build a much-needed high school for the fast growing Parkdale area. The Sisters had to act quickly. The girls were relocated to the St. Vincent Residence on Sackville Street, then to R.J. Fleming's estate at Bathurst and St. Clair. The boys would remain in part of the orphanage while another section was rapidly converted into hospital, a use that was not subject to the expropriation laws of the day. And so it was that on October 19, 1921, 75 years ago last Friday, Cornelius Murphy was admitted, becoming the first patient to be cared for in Toronto's new twenty-four-bed St. Joseph's Hospital.

Over the years St. Joe's has provided a full range of medical and surgical services, paediatrics, obstetrics, and psychiatric care. Introduced in 1931 the various clinics, where health-care services were made available regardless of the patient's ability to pay (a concept initiated years before government-funded hospitalization became the norm) continue to serve the community to this day. One such service is the Family Medicine Clinic, which was often frequented by illegal immigrants and destitute refugees, most of whom have no medical coverage or hope of ever being able to afford treatment that is frequently life-saving. Those founding four Sisters of 1851 would be proud. Other highlight's of St. Joseph's seventy-five-year history include:

> 1921 – School of Nursing founded.
> 1949 – opening of the paediatrics unit (the city's first, other than the unit at the Hospital for Sick Children).
> 1960 – construction of the Glendale Wing, increasing bed capacity to 600.
> 1962 – Toronto's first intensive care Unit opened.
> 1965 – initiation of the Respiratory Home Care Program — another Toronto first.
> 1984 – "cat scan" service introduced.

We can only hope that the government in all its wisdom leaves well enough alone.

COLISEUM TURNS 75

October 27, 1996

At 11:30 am on Tuesday, November 5, 1996 visitors to this year's Royal Agricultural Winter Fair will be invited to watch as Prince Phillip unveils a new Toronto Historical Board plaque that commemorates the seventy-fifth anniversary of the opening of the Coliseum in 1921. This sprawling landmark at the east end of Exhibition Place, a structure that will soon become a major component of the ultra-modern National Trade Centre, was originally conceived as the home of the newly organized Royal Winter Fair.

The genesis of the fair itself can be traced to the years prior to the outbreak of the Great War when several gentlemen with agricultural interests sought a way in which the various segments of Canadian agriculture could be showcased. Using Guelph's annual Ontario Provincial Winter Fair and the Ottawa Winter Fair as examples, along with the extremely popular International Live Stock Exposition held in Chicago, their dream was realized

Opened in 1921, the seventy-five-year-old Coliseum will be honoured with a Toronto Historical Board plaque to be unveiled by Prince Philip during this year's Royal Winter Fair.

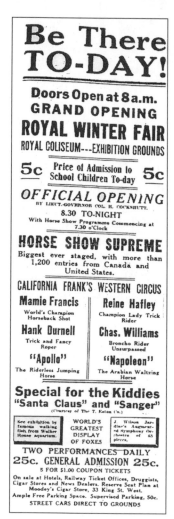

Be There TO-DAY!

Doors Open at 8 a.m.

GRAND OPENING

ROYAL WINTER FAIR

ROYAL COLISEUM---EXHIBITION GROUNDS

5c Price of Admission to
School Children To-day **5c**

OFFICIAL OPENING

BY LIEUT.-GOVERNOR COL. H. COCKSHUTT.

8.30 TO-NIGHT

With Horse Show Programme Commencing at
7.30 o'Clock

HORSE SHOW SUPREME

Biggest ever staged, with more than
1,200 entries from Canada and
United States.

CALIFORNIA FRANK'S WESTERN CIRCUS

Mamie Francis	**Reine Hafley**
World's Champion Horseback Shot	Champion Lady Trick Rider
Hank Durnell	**Chas. Williams**
Trick and Fancy Roper	Broncho Rider Unsurpassed
"Apollo"	**"Napoleon"**
The Riderless Jumping Horse	The Arabian Waltzing Horse

Special for the Kiddies
"Santa Claus" and "Sanger"
(Courtesy of The T. Eaton Co.)

See exhibition by famous walking fish from Walker House aquarium.	WORLD'S GREATEST DISPLAY OF FOXES	J. Wilson Jardine's Augmented Symphony Orchestra of 45 pieces.

TWO PERFORMANCES DAILY
25c. GENERAL ADMISSION 25c.

5 FOR $1.00 COUPON TICKETS

On sale at Hotels, Railway Ticket Offices, Druggists, Cigar Stores and News Dealers. Reserve Seat Plan at Moodey's Cigar Store, 33 King St. West. Ample Free Parking Space. Supervised Parking, 50c.

STREET CARS DIRECT TO GROUNDS

Newspaper ad for the first
Royal Winter Fair in 1922.

with the National Live Stock and Dairy Show that was held in Toronto in 1913. But a call to arms the following year and a seemingly endless world war resulted in that event being a one-time affair.

However, when victory finally seemed in sight, plans were revived for a truly national agricultural show — a show that would include competitive classes for all breeds of livestock and varieties of produce from all the provinces. Soon after the war ended the decision was made that the time was now right to once again pursue the idea of a national agricultural winter fair. A series of meetings were held, the most important of which convened in the Royal Connaught Hotel in Hamilton on October 28, 1919. It was here that the site of the new fair was selected. In the running were the Ontario cities of London, Hamilton, and, of course, Toronto.

Soon only Hamilton and Toronto were being considered and both of these communities presented strong arguments as to why they should be chosen. The key seemed to be Toronto's offer to provide a site on the Exhibition grounds *and* a new $1-million building in which the fair could be held. Nevertheless, when the delegates cast their ballots to determine the site of the proposed winter fair, each city received exactly eighteen votes. It was then up to W.A. Dryden, the committee chairman, to break the tie, which he did by casting his vote in favour of the provincial capital. Toronto's Royal Agricultural Winter Fair was born.

The million-dollar building that had been proposed by the city turned out to be today's Coliseum, although in the early design phases — and even when the cornerstone was laid on July 27, 1921 — it was known as the Live Stock Arena, or simply the Arena.

There was every hope that the massive structure would be ready in time for the first Royal Agricultural Winter Fair, which was scheduled to open in late November of that same year, 1921. However, for a variety of reasons, including the fact that all one million dollars had been spent before a heating plant had been built, that wasn't to be. When it was announced that the fair would have to be postponed a year the committee went, to use a modern expression, ballistic. "Without heat the guests wouldn't be able to appear in their evening clothes, but would have to wear coonskin coats," thundered one committee member. "And the city's idea of installing 70 or more stoves as a temporary measure would mean that some of the show cattle and most of the prize poultry would be roasted during the fair rather than after."

In spite of the obvious disappointment, the first Royal Winter Fair had to be postponed. The first Royal didn't open until November 22, 1922. Somehow the question of inadequate heat was settled and the Coliseum, although built for the presentation of the first Royal Agricultural Winter Fair, actually opened on December 21, 1921 with an athletic program sponsored by the Sportsmen's Patriotic Association. So while the Coliseum is seventy-five years old this year, the Royal won't celebrate its seventy-fifth until 1997. Interestingly, when the Arena — oops, Coliseum — opened it was the largest exhibit building under one roof in the world.

Work on the new Live Stock Arena (soon to be renamed the Royal Coliseum, then simply the Coliseum) is well along in this fall, 1921 photo.

THEY'RE TORONTO "FIRSTS"

November 3, 1996

The city's newspapers for November 1, 1945, fifty-one years ago last Friday, featured reports covering two totally different subjects, each of which would enter the history books as a "Toronto first." Unfortunately, they were also of the "I have some good news" and "I have some bad news" variety. Let's do the bad news first and put it out of the way.

Halloween Eve, fifty-one years ago, was the first time in many long years that the evening could be celebrated without the spectre of war, death, and destruction hovering over what was supposed to be a night of simple tricks and pleasant treats. Ever since the outbreak of hostilities in 1939, each succeeding year's All Hallows' Eve was greeted with less and less enthusiasm as the news from the front grew more and more melancholy. Now that the war was over and the enemy had been vanquished, a few of the more rambunctious Torontonians believed that with the arrival of Halloween, 1945

The scene of raucous rioting on Halloween, 1945, the former Main Street Police Station is now a quiet community centre.

it was time to go a little crazy. And, perhaps not coincidentally, the fact that many city policemen hadn't as yet returned to civilian duty made that idea even more tempting. While a few minor occurrences disturbed the peace in various parts of town, as well out in the farm fields of North York, Scarborough, and Etobicoke townships, real problems were brewing out Queen Street East. About 9 pm several small bonfires were set at the intersection of Queen and Hammersmith, and before long others were blazing at intersections as far east as Maclean Avenue. Naturally, the police were called and, after assessing the situation, appealed to the large crowds of young people that had gathered to disperse. When the firemen from Main Street station arrived on the scene to dowse flames, which were now being fed by wood ripped from nearby fences and threatening several of the buildings along Queen, the crowd really got out of control. Large wooden boxes were thrown in front of the fire truck. Them some fool poured gasoline onto the streetcar tracks and threw in a match, and suddenly the night glowed brightly as ribbons of flame raced along Queen Street towards an approaching streetcar. Police reinforcements were called in, including a young Jack Webster (now the Police Services Historian at the fascinating police museum, located on the main floor of Police Headquarters, 40 College Street) who had just returned from overseas and was working out of old Cowan Avenue station. Also on the scene were members of the mounted unit. Several of the more boisterous members of the crowd were placed under arrest and transported to #10 Police Station up on Main Street. This was when things really got out of hand as a huge mob, estimated by some sources as numbering at least seven thousand, marched on the station in an attempt to free their pals. Suddenly rocks, bricks, and bottles were sent flying as the mob attacked the station. Just south of #10 was (and still is) #22 Fire Hall. To protect the policemen, and themselves, the firemen broke out the hoses and showered the frenzied crowd in an attempt to drive them back. Numerous windows were shattered and several police and firemen were injured. Finally, for the first time in living memory, Acting Police Chief John Chisholm read the "Riot Act." That, plus the arrival of additional police reinforcements and a few more arrests, resulted in the mob eventually dispersing. The rest of the evening saw only scattered incidents throughout the neighbourhood, but the worst part of the evening had passed. Of course, as with just about any event of this nature, the cops took the brunt of the attack only to have those doing the attacking complain, when it was all over, that there had been police brutality. Not surprisingly, there's no record of the police protesting incidents of mob brutality.

* * * * *

F/L Jack Ritch (right) and F/L Bill MacKenzie in front of the "squirt," the newspaper's name for the revolutionary Gloster *Meteor*.

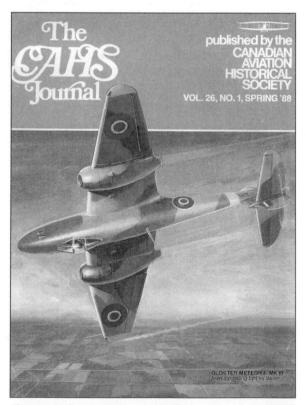

The revolutionary Meteor graced the cover of the CAHS Journal spring 1968.

The following morning a much less destructive "Toronto first" took place when former Danforth Tech student Jack Ritch piloted his Gloster *Meteor* over the city. The revolutionary *Meteor*, on its way to Alberta where it would undergo cold weather testing, appeared over several southern Ontario cities, as well as being placed on display out at Malton Airport. As the plane streaked over Bloor Street and the Danforth Jack's family, friends, and school chums gathered on front porches and rooftops to witness history in the making. For the vast majority of Torontonians this was the first time they had ever seen a jet-propelled airplane. In fact, the daily newspapers were at such a loss for words to describe the innovative new *Meteor* that they simply referred to it as the "squirt," an obvious reference to the hot gases rushing out the jet's tailpipe and propelled the propellerless aircraft through the sky.

During the war Jack was one of only two RCAF pilots assigned to the Royal Air Force's 616 Squadron where he flew the *Meteor*, the only allied jet to see action in the Second World War. With its exceptional (for the time) speed the *Meteor* was responsible for the destruction of seventeen of Germany's feared V-1 "buzz-bombs." Jack got one of those seventeen simply by flying beside it, lifting its wing, and tipping it over. Jack now lives in Scarborough.

Readers interested in learning more about our country's fascinating aviation history (including the *Meteor* story) are encouraged to join the Canadian Aviation Historical Society. Membership details can be obtained by writing the CAHS-Toronto Chapter, c/o Suite 3710, 85 Thorncliffe Park Dr., Toronto M4H 1L6.

Road Name Honours War Dead

November 10, 1996

For my Remembrance Day column two years ago I submitted an article that featured several streets in Metro Toronto, each of which had been named to honour either a group of Canadian soldiers (Warvet Crescent in East York, for example, venerates all Canadian war veterans), an individual who had won the coveted Victoria Cross (Topham Road for Corporal Fred Topham VC, Hornell Avenue for Flight Lieutenant David Hornell VC), the medal itself (Vicross Road) or for prominent battles in which Canadians participated. Of this latter variety there are numerous examples in the city directory, Courcelette Road, Vimy Avenue, Falaise Road, Abbeville Road, Dunkirk Road, Normandy Boulevard, to name just a few. In the 1994 column I briefly described the first engagement included in this list, the Battle of Courcelette, not realizing that subsequent research would reveal a story that identifies this street with our community in a much more meaningful way.

Courcelette is a small village in northern France near the River Somme. It was here on February 15, 1916 that members of the Second and Third divisions fought a fierce battle, eventually wrestling control of this sector away from the battle-hardened German army. An important new piece of military hardware was used for the first time in this battle, but as the term "tank" (the word having been selected to ensure the secrecy of the new weapon) had yet to be used, the author of the following newspaper item was forced to use the description "armoured cars" to enable the readers at home to follow the event more easily.

> The morning of September 15 dawned bright and clear. There was a frosty nip in the air. Suddenly our massed artillery burst into a frenzy of activity. Shells of every calibre were hurled over the heads of the waiting infantry. Shortly after six our battalions began their attack. Before them the artillery barrage advanced stage by stage with a remarkable precision and a great intensity of fire. In successive waves our infantry moved forward, climbing over the shell-torn

ground, leaping the battered trenches. Among them burst the enemy's shells The noise was terrific. Machine gun and rifle fire poured into them. Steadily they mounted the last ridge, saw Martinpuich on their right and looked over to the brick ruins and white chalk mounds of the sugar refinery. The trenches to the right and left were to be their objective. No sooner were the first lines of German trenches secured than the assaulting waves pressed onwards. In their midst, moving ponderously and with great determination, came several of the new armoured cars. The effect upon our men was electrical. In vain, the enemy rained a stream of bullets against the invulnerable cars. They were powerless to stop their advance. Although our infantry waves were the first to reach the sugar refinery the cars assisted materially in silencing the German machine guns. The 15th was a memorable day for Canada.

The **Canadian Army in Action**
and the
Advance of the Tanks

THE OFFICIAL MOVING PICTURES OF THE BATTLE OF COURCELETTE AND THE FIRST INTRODUCTION OF THE BRITISH TANKS, ISSUED TO THE PEOPLE OF CANADA BY THE CANADIAN WAR RECORDS OFFICE IN COMMON TRIBUTE TO THOSE OF HER SONS WHO FOUGHT TO VICTORY AND TO THOSE WHO DIED VICTORIOUS, AND TO BE A LIVING RECORD IN THE NATIONAL ARCHIVES OF CANADA FOR ALL TIME.

These Pictures are to be presented in Toronto all next week by Jule and Jay J. Allen at the Regent Theatre, from 10 a.m. to 11 p.m. continuously each day, starting Monday

Afternoons : Balcony and Ground Floor, 25c ; Loges, 35c—Regent Theatre—Evenings : Balcony, 25c ; Ground Floor, 35c ; Loges, 50

During the course of the heavy fighting many of the enemy were killed or wounded, with more than 1,200 taken prisoner — a figure that included thirty-two officers. But what the article failed to report (no doubt as a result of strict censorship) was the fact that the Canadians too suffered numerous casualties. Of those who were killed in the action in and around the small French village six were residents of Scarborough Township, and in a strange twist of fate all six lived on the same street. Harry Guest, Peter Barr, Sam Bamblett, Bert Wallwork, Richard Hinshaw, and Howard Crabbe, young men all, eagerly entered the service and proudly served their country — a country to which they would never return. To honour their memories the township council changed the name of their street, Chester Avenue, to Courcelette Road.

Amongst Bert Wallwork's possessions was a small autograph book in which were penned these few lines;

When the cannons are roaring,
And colours are flying,
The lads who seek honor,
Must never fear dying.

* * * * *

Those who were lucky enough to survive the carnage of the so-called "war to end all wars," but required special attention as a result of injuries sustained during the four years of conflict, were often admitted to the Military Orthopaedic Hospital that opened in 1919 in the former National Cash Register factory on Christie Street. For a time patients in this treatment facility included not only victims of the Great War, but a few South African War (1899–1902) and Fenian Raid (1866) veterans as well. In 1936 the name was changed to the Christie Street Veterans' Hospital. Even though attempts were made to continue using the old hospital for the Second World War's returning wounded, a tremendous public outcry against the aging old building ultimately forced the construction of a new hospital in North York Township. The new facility Sunnybrook Military Hospital on Bayview Avenue, opened on June 12, 1948. The Christie Street Hospital became Lambert Lodge, a seniors' home named in honour of Padre Lt. Col. Sidney Lambert, a veteran of both world wars. The structure was demolished in 1981.

On November 12, 1996 a commemorative Toronto Historical Board plaque was unveiled at the Christie Gardens Apartments, 600 Melita Crescent, site of the Christie Street Veteran's Hospital.

CURTAIN'S UP ON THEATRE IN OLD T.O.

November 17, 1996

Stan Laurel as he appeared when he played Toronto's Loew's Theatre in 1920.

A look at the entertainment pages of the city's various newspapers will quickly reveal just how wealthy this town is when it comes to the presentation of the latest in motion pictures and the best in live theatre. While this may seem like a recent phenomenon, historically Toronto has always enjoyed a special status in the world of entertainment. Research indicates that as early as 1820 citizens of the young community (in existence for only twenty-seven years and still fourteen years away from becoming a city) were being entertained in the ballroom located on the second floor of Frank's Hotel at the northwest corner of Colborne Street and West Market Lane. The evening's entertainment was provided by a small American theatrical company that took pride in presenting the day's most popular plays including works such as *Ali Baba, The Lady of the Lake,* and *Pizarro.*

The idea of "going to the theatre" obviously caught on and over the years the city saw the opening of a multitude of live theatre playhouses, including such divergent venues as the Royal Lyceum, Grand Opera House, Royal Opera House, Albert Hall, Shaftsbury Hall, and the Masonic Hall on Toronto Street.

Coincident with the arrival of the new century, burlesque and vaudeville arrived in Toronto and once again performers from south of the border as well as others from "over 'ome," made a bee line for this city eager to strut their stuff on the stages of the many new theatres built specifically for this new form of diversion. One of the most popular playhouses was the Strand on the east side of Yonge just north of King. It was here that a multitude of "musical pantomimists," "dancing comedians," "comedy jugglers," "dancing dogs," and "rubber-faced comics" enthralled audiences that couldn't get enough. One week the theatre even featured a couple of guys described as "acromedians." Don't ask.

Even though the Strand was a relatively small theatre it was large enough to accommodate "4 live, breathing, plunging Arabian horses driven by daredevil drivers at breakneck speed right on the Strand stage," or so a November, 1920 newspaper ad promised. Other theatres like the Tivoli, Shea's, Loew's, and Pantages were built — all much larger than the Strand. In fact, Pantages was (and remains) the city's largest. It was at the Loew's (now the Elgin) during the week of April 3, 1920 that a couple, fresh from the English music hall stage, appeared in a skit titled "No Mother to Guide Him." Although the billing suggested that they were married, in fact they were not — not legally that is. Her real name was Mae Dahlberg while her partner, with whom she both worked and lived, had been christened Stanley Jefferson. Concerned that his surname had thirteen letters Stanley changed it — on Mae's suggestion — to a name by which he would become world famous. Two years after leaving Mae, Stan teamed up with a rotund American-born comedian and in 1927 they made the first of the ever-popular Laurel and Hardy films.

Loew's playbill for the week of April 3, 1920. Note Stan Laurel's name (along with that of his stage partner and "wife" Mae) at bottom right.

LOEW'S
HIGH CLASS VAUDEVILLE · FEATURE PHOTO PRODUCTIONS
WEEK APRIL 5th   PHONE MAIN 3600—401 FOR SEAT RESERVATION

The Screen's Most Brilliant and Versatile Actress
NORMA TALMADGE
In a Wonderful Picturization of LeRoy Scott's Novel
"A Daughter Of Two Worlds"
Imagine the opportunity for fine acting in this romance of Jennie Malone, daughter of an inhabitant of the slums, who, defying the clinging clutch of undesirable associates, pursued and persecuted by the police, still rises superior to her birth and environment to an honored place in society and wins the love and respect of a splendid man.

| Jack and Tommy Weir | Butter and De Muth |
| Offer "At the Races" | Harmony and Eccentric Bits |

BERNARD & MYERS   In a Laugh Treat "The Cabby and the Fare"

| Russell and Devitt | Stan and Mae Laurel |
| Entertainers and Acromedians | "No Mother to Guide Him" |

"SWEET SWEETIES"
Featuring Billy Barnes, Jack Barton and Rene Braham.
Reinforced by a Dash of Broadway's Bewitching Femininity.

WINTER GARDEN
SAME PERFORMANCE AS LOEW'S
EVERY EVENING AT 7.30. ALL SEATS RESERVED. SEAT ORDERS HELD TILL 6.30 P.M.

While on the subject of live

theatre, one of the most enjoyable musical presentations to be seen in Toronto in a long time will finally wrap up this coming December 31. A night at *Forever Plaid* is certainly a night full of nostalgia and fun. Interestingly, several of the songs featured in the show were made popular by "guy groups" from right here in Toronto: the *Four Lads* ("No, Not Much," "Moments to Remember") and the Crew Cuts ("Crazy 'Bout Ya Baby").

* * * * *

With all this commotion about whether the City of Toronto as we now know it will continue to exist following the November, 1997 municipal elections the owners of small businesses, uncertain as to which of the dozens of regulatory proclamations will still be in force, must be going nuts. For instance, which of the various "you can smoke up there, or down there but not over here" by-laws will they be expected to follow is anyone's guess. But, as a reader reminded me in a recent letter, this type of confusion is not new. Carman's, now one of Toronto's most popular restaurants, was faced with a similar bureaucratic predicament when it first opened in 1959, except back then the rule that had the struggling young owner baffled was the one that stated that it was unlawful to serve liquor except in a private club. So what did Arthur Carman do? Of course, he turned the place into a private club complete with a mandatory membership requirement. For the next sixteen years Carman's Club sold more than 25,000 memberships at $2 each with all the money garnered being turned over to the Variety Club.

IMAGES OF OUR PAST CAPTURED ON VIDEO

December 15, 1996

J ust about everyone is intrigued with old photographs, especially the ones that show areas of our city with which we are familiar. Places like the waterfront when the ferry docks were west of the foot of Bay Street, the amusement park at Hanlan's Point, the little picnic grove that straddled a little creek flowing under a dusty Sheppard/Leslie intersection, the little airport on the west side of Dufferin Street just south of today's sprawling Yorkdale mall — the list can go on forever.

While old black-and-white still photos are great to look at, you can imagine how much more exciting it is to watch early views of our city come to life as they do in a new video put together by transportation buff Ray Neilson to celebrate the seventy-fifth anniversary of the TTC. Titled "The TTC Story, the Video," this fascinating production includes rare scenes of the city prior to the introduction of TTC service in 1921, vintage footage of TTC streetcars and buses rushing through city streets in the early years of its mandate (much of this footage in colour), plus a selection of "home movies" featuring various parts of the city taken by a multitude of people long before video cameras became commonplace. A short trip into the countryside on a beautiful old Gray Coach bus, a run up Yonge Street on a radial car, the introduction and demise of the environmentally friendly trolley bus, and many, many more facets of our city's transportation history can be seen in "The TTC Story, the Video." It's 120 minutes in length, sells for $40 and is available from George's Trains on Mt. Pleasant Road or by mail from GPS Video, P.O. Box 5895, Stn. "A", Toronto M5W 1P3 (in the latter case $40 includes all taxes and mailing charges).

While reviewing the video it became quite evident that this production is not just for transit fans, but would be a great addition to any nostalgia buff's video library since incorporated into some of the street scenes are long demolished buildings while in the foreground dozens of now-classic automobiles race hither, thither and yon.

While the two photos that accompany this column are not from the video they graphically illustrate what else besides transit vehicles can be found in old views of the city, whether they're of the still photo or motion picture variety.

TTC crews busily at work replacing streetcar rails on St. Clair Avenue West near the corner of what was Ossington Avenue and is now Winona Drive. Note the Red Indian and White Rose gasoline stations in the centre background and the curbside gas pump to the extreme left. The large billboard promotes the Toronto-built Willys-Knight automobile.

In one of the photos we see work crews busily removing the private streetcar right-of-way that had been constructed in the centre of St. Clair Avenue in 1911–13 and on which the city operated the *St. Clair* cars of the pioneer Toronto Civic Railways, one of several companies absorbed by the TTC when the latter went into business in 1921. The right-of-way's removal was undertaken by the Commission during the Great Depression as a "make work" project. Having dropped off passengers at Ossington Avenue (now Winona Drive), one of the TTC's many "wooden" streetcars emerges from behind the steam shovel. On the north side of St. Clair several autos squeeze by a TTC work truck. And speaking of cars, on the billboard we see an ad for a Willys-Knight Standard Six automobile that was on sale at Crang's Garage for $1,395. The Willys-Overland Company of Toledo, Ohio entered Canada in 1914 and relocated from Hamilton to the old Russell car factory on Weston Road in late 1915. The company moved to Windsor in 1934, was purchased by Henry Kaiser in 1953, and ceased auto production in Canada altogether when acquired by American Motors in 1970.

To show just how recent our past is in this city, the day after this column ran a reader called to say he lived in the building to which the billboard was attached, and that may be his sister watching the workmen

LONG-STANDING HOUSES OF WORSHIP

December 22, 1996

No, dear reader, you're not looking at pictures of the same church taken from different angles. They are, in fact, two different houses of worship located miles apart, but both overlook Yonge Street and both were designed by the same man, John George Howard — a well-known architect and the "warden of High Park."

The older of the two structures — and only by a few months — is Christ Church in Holland Landing. It had been erected to serve the spiritual needs of the adherents to the Church of England faith, who lived in and around this pretty little community on Highway 11 several miles north of Metro. In the early years of the last century, Holland Landing was a busy place, situated as it was at the northern terminus of the original thirty-four-mile stretch of a dusty (except following downpours when it was the opposite, muddy) Yonge Street. People travelling from the lakes in the hinterland to the north and east and bound for Toronto (called York until 1834) would make the long journey by boat via the Trent or Severn waterways into Lake Simcoe (named by Governor Simcoe to honour his father), then down the Holland River (its name recognizes Major General Samuel Holland, Surveyor General of Canada), disembarking at its junction with the governor's "great" military and communications thoroughfare, Yonge Street, where the journey to the small capital would continue by cart, coach, horseback, or on foot.

Christ Church, Holland Landing

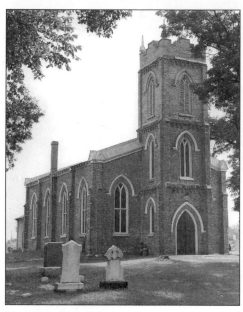
St. John's, York Mills

Travel in the opposite direction was equally busy and by the 1870s Holland Landing had grown into a thriving community of some seven hundred citizens. And with many (if not all) of those souls in need of salvation, a new church became a community necessity. And so it was that Christ Church was to open its doors in 1843.

At about the same time the other church pictured here was under construction about twenty-five miles to the south, although it wasn't to be consecrated until the following year. Called St. John's, York Mills, it replaced the small frame structure where Anglicans living in the vicinity of the mills north of York had been worshipping for the past several years.

Back in those days, the alignment of Yonge Street in this part of York Township was significantly different from that of today. The deep ravine through which the west branch of the Don River flows, Hogg's Hollow (so-named by the Hogg brothers, early settlers and land developers, in honour of their father John Hogg), was virtually impassible for horse-drawn wagons and carts. To allow for easier passage through the ravine, surveyors deflected Yonge Street to the east of its initial alignment. Today that realignment can be traced by following Donwoods Drive, Donino Avenue, and Old Yonge Street. Thus, when the original St. John's was built in 1817, it sat west of Yonge Street. Today, the church sits to the east of a much, much busier Yonge Street. Incidentally, the realignment project was described by Dr. Henry Scadding, the city's learned historian of years gone by, as being one which "the ancient Roman road-makers would have deemed most respectable."

Both churches were the work of John George Howard. Born John Corby in Hertfordshire, England in 1803 (the reason for the name change has never been fully expalined), Howard emigrated to York in 1832. Thanks to the lieutenant-governor of the day, Sir John Colborne, he was appointed drawing master at Upper Canada, which was still located at the corner of King and Simcoe streets. Several years later, when Howard constructed a residence on

John George Howard (1803–1890)

his rambling property well out in the countryside west of the city, he called it Colborne Lodge in tribute to his mentor.

In addition to being an accomplished architect, Howard also did engineering and surveying work. In fact, he surveyed the young city's first sidewalks and laid out St. James' Cemetery when the grave yard was relocated well to the north of the church.

In 1873, in return for annual pension of $1,200, Howard agreed to bequeath is High Park property to the citizens of Toronto on his death. Howard lived to be 87, so the 120-acre park (which many believe he gave to Toronto) actually cost the taxpayer almost $20,000. Still quite a bargain!